Yourself

Start Your Own Business In A Week

Kevin Duncan

First published in Great Britain in 2013 by Hodder & Stoughton. An Hachette UK company.

This edition published in 2016 by John Murray Learning

British Library Cataloguing in Publication Data: a catalogue record for this title is available from the British Library.

Library of Congress Catalog Card Number: on file.

ISBN: 978 1 473 60936 5

eISBN: 978 1 444 18599 7

1

The publisher has used its best endeavours to ensure that any website addresses referred to in this book are correct and active at the time of going to press. However, the publisher and the author have no responsibility for the websites and can make no guarantee that a site will remain live or that the content will remain relevant, decent or appropriate.

The publisher has made every effort to mark as such all words which it believes to be trademarks. The publisher should also like to make it clear that the presence of a word in the book, whether marked or unmarked, in no way affects its legal status as a trademark.

Every reasonable effort has been made by the publisher to trace the copyright holders of material in this book. Any errors or omissions should be notified in writing to the publisher, who will endeavour to rectify the situation for any reprints and future editions.

Typeset by Cenveo® Publisher Services.

Printed and bound in Great Britain by CPI Group (UK) Ltd, Croydon, CR0 4YY.

John Murray Learning policy is to use papers that are natural, renewable and recyclable products and made from wood grown in sustainable forests. The logging and manufacturing processes are expected to conform to the environmental regulations of the country of origin.

John Murray Learning
Carmelite House
50 Victoria Embankment
London EC4Y 0DZ
www.hodder.co.uk

Contents

Introduction	2
Sunday	4
Getting started	
Monday	22
The right tools for the job	
Tuesday	38
Getting the money right	
Wednesday	54
Communicating effectively	
Thursday	70
Taming the telephone	
Friday	86
How to conduct yourself	
Saturday	102
Setting up reminders and tripwires	
7 × 7	116
Answers	122

Introduction

We owe it to ourselves to make our working life enjoyable, even if the main reason for it is to make money. The central principle of this book is that starting your own business can be the best feeling in the world. Free of the constraints of company life, and brimming with enthusiasm at the prospect of at last being able to realize the benefits of your own idea, you are all set to experience the thrill of being your own boss.

When you start your own business, you have total responsibility – that's right, *total responsibility*. The glory is all yours when things go well, and of course the problems are all yours when they don't. Therefore, as well as being a hugely rewarding experience, it can also be a very scary state of affairs – a world where there never seems to *be* a weekend because you can't stop thinking about a problem or fretting over where the next payment is coming from.

People who run their own business are used to the reaction 'You work for yourself? That's great', but many walk away from such a conversation thinking, 'If only they knew the headaches involved.' However, with a sound business idea and the right approach, millions have already shown that you can definitely run a successful business and have a better-balanced personal life as a result. That means a much fairer equation between the effort you put in and the reward you get out, whether that's financial or emotional.

Being organized, thinking ahead, and learning to switch off are some of the qualities that those who start their own business must master, whether they use their home as an office or run their own business from a shop or workshop. Being your own boss does not mean that you are destined to feel lonely or isolated: more people than ever before are now working from home and have found ways to ensure that they still see people during the working day.

This book is intended for anyone who has decided to start their own business. It is designed to be your business companion. Running your own business is all about self-confidence. It's essential that you believe that you are good at what you do. Equally, you will never be perfect; so don't beat yourself up if you don't do everything that this book suggests, or if you do some things differently.

Do it your way and make it work for you, because that's what running your own business is all about.

Kevin Duncan

SUNDAY

Getting started

It's a daunting prospect, isn't it? An empty desk, no customers, no confirmed money coming in, and no one to gossip with. Welcome to running your own business! Every issue is now yours to wrestle with, and yours alone. But then so is all the satisfaction – mental and financial – when things are going well. Today we are going to work out exactly how you are going to turn what many would regard as an ordeal into the start of a fantastic success.

We are going to look at:

- how to be honest with yourself about your offer
- what you need to prepare in order to be a success
- how to write a simple, realistic plan
- working out the materials that you need
- how to get it all under way.

Assume that you have something to offer

Let's start by assuming that there is a market for your talents; otherwise you wouldn't have got this far. We have to believe that this is true because you probably wouldn't be reading this book unless you were convinced that you have something to offer. By now you will have established the basics in your mind. Your thought pattern will have been something along the lines of:

- I am good at what I do.
- I believe that there is a market for my product or service. (Whether this is actually true, and how you set about proving it to yourself, will come a little later.)
- I can do my job better on my own than in my current set-up.
- I have a way of doing my job that people will like.
- What I put in alongside what I get out will be a better-balanced equation than my current state of affairs.

Thousands of people go through this thought process at some point in their working lives – sometimes on many occasions. However, even if you have been able to tick all the boxes so far, the issue that you have to grapple with next is far more fundamental: 'If I ran my own business, I'm not sure if I could live with myself.'

When people say this, they mean that they are thinking about important issues such as where exactly they are going to do their work and what their domestic arrangements are. Could they possibly accommodate getting everything done that they need to without disrupting all the other aspects of their life?

Secondly, there is your frame of mind: are you cut out to operate outside a conventional office environment? Could you cope without the interaction? Could you motivate yourself when no one is giving you a kick up the backside? It is essential that you feel good about yourself and what you have to offer.

TIP

Feel good about your offer

You must genuinely believe that you can offer something of value to others; otherwise you should not take the plunge to start up on your own, or even be toying with the idea.

Be honest with yourself

Do remember, however, that confidence can be misplaced. In fact, over-confidence could beguile you into believing that you have a viable idea or a successful way of doing things when in fact you don't, so confront your own hubris and work it out privately before it trips you up.

You are starting your own business now, so you shouldn't have to pretend about anything. In fact, you mustn't ever stray into the realms of fantasy, because you would only be fooling yourself if you did. From now on it is your job to be sensible and realistic. Don't exaggerate your potential or delude yourself that you can do all sorts of things that you cannot. Equally, do not be sheepish about your skills. You will need to get used to showing a fascinating blend of confidence and humility.

Consider your position with extreme care and as much objectivity as you can muster. Get a piece of paper. Write down what you want to do in your business. Stare at it for a bit, and then decide whether anyone else would agree with you. This is the beginning of establishing whether there is indeed a market for what you do. Go for a walk. When you come back, stare at your piece of paper again. Is your idea any good? Is it nonsense? If so, write a new one. Stick it on the wall and live with it for a few days. Does it still make sense? Is it rubbish? Does everyone else claim the same thing? What's so different about the way that you would run your business? These early enquiries are really important.

Research your market thoroughly

If you reckon you have an excellent idea, the first essential thing to do is to research your market thoroughly. Actually it isn't one thing to do – it's a lot of things. Try asking yourself these sorts of questions:

- What demand is there for what I provide?
  - If I am producing a product, who wants to buy it?
  - If I am providing a service, who needs it?
- Who else in the area does this already? (This could be geographical or sector-based.)
  - Are they a success? If so, why?
  - Are they a failure? If so, what does that tell me?
- What price can I put on my product or service?
  - Does that represent a going concern or will I be hard-pushed to make a living?
- What outside factors am I subject to?
  - Can I influence these factors, or am I totally at their mercy?
  - If I have no control over them, does that make the whole venture too vulnerable?
- If I were someone else, would I embark on this venture?
  - If so, why?

The questions are endless, but try to be like an inquisitive child and always ask *why?* three times in relation to every question.

Work out how much money you need

What is required here is not a forest of spreadsheets but just a really clear impression of how your business will work financially. Put simply, there are three types of money that you will need:

1 Initial investment
2 Monthly cash flow
3 The profit margin

Initial investment

Do you need to put any money in at all at the beginning? Just pause on this one for a moment. If the answer is no, then don't do it.

If you do need to borrow from some other source, what demands will they make on getting it back? Banks want interest. Investors want cash back. They don't do it out of kindness.

If you really do conclude that you have to put money in yourself, when are you going to get it back? Don't delude yourself by excluding this amount from your assessment of whether the business is going to be a success.

Monthly cash flow

Next comes the monthly cash flow or the amount of income you need each month. Write down what you need. Now write down what you think you can get. Then build in time delays for late payment in the early days. This becomes your first cash flow projection. This has to be very, very realistic. You have to have a reasonable level of confidence that it is achievable otherwise you will have a disaster on your hands almost straight away. You need to distinguish carefully between income and profit. Income is not profit. You can have an infinite amount of income and yet still be making a whopping loss.

Calculate how much you need to make each month. Once you write it down, it's more likely to happen. You can have a sensible minimum and maximum, but it's better if you have just one figure. Now you have to work out where it's coming from. Write down a realistic list of the value of your income in the first three months. If this turns out to be nonsense, write a more realistic list next time. As you become better at predicting this, you will naturally build in time lags to reflect slow decision-making and slow payment.

The profit margin

The third thing is the profit margin. Ask yourself:

- How much is it?
- Does it vary depending on what I've sold?
- Does it vary by month or season?
- Does it fluctuate wildly and, if so, why?
- What would make it more consistent?
- What would make it higher?
- What are the tolerance levels?
- What is the average target?
- Is that realistic?
- Is it good enough for me?

You need to keep a regular and close eye on this. You also need to have decided whether you need the margin monthly, annually, or over any other time period.

If you need it monthly, does this mean that your business plan does not include an amount for your own salary? If so, consider whether that is wise or realistic.

If you can take the profit annually, how are you keeping tabs on the surplus that you hope is building up? Can you equate it back to the running monthly amount?

The overall rule is to keep all this very simple.

Write a simple, realistic plan

Quite a few people starting a business write endless business plans before they start, and there's nothing fundamentally wrong with that. However, it's easy to get so involved in the spreadsheets and the financial projections of a plan that you lose sight of the basics. The best business plans can often be written on the back of an envelope, usually in your local café or bar. Try this simple process:

1 Write JFMAMJJASOND along the top of the page to represent the 12 months of the year.
2 Now cross out at least one or two of them because you will be taking some holiday and in the first year the whole thing will probably grind to a halt when you are not around.
3 Now write a figure under each month to determine your income.
4 Put the likely costs under each.
5 Subtract one from the other and see what you have left.
6 If you want to be particularly cautious, try crossing out the first three months' income because businesses always take longer to get off the ground than you think.
7 Now go and do something else for a while.
8 Come back to your plan and ask yourself again: 'Is this realistic?'

This exercise will tell you something a great deal more fundamental than a meeting with the bank or your accountant. It will be a big surprise if you are happy with it first time. In fact, if you are, you should be a bit suspicious. Live with it for a while. Try again. Make refinements (not on a spreadsheet, just in pen on another envelope). The great joy with this is that, by keeping it simple, you are now able to explain your business plan to anyone who will listen – and that includes you. Now, assuming that you have concluded that you do indeed have a going concern, there are some things that you will need to get under way.

Invest in a distinctive identity

You need to look good. Your company, shop or service needs a memorable name, a good logo, high-quality headed paper, good-quality signage and business cards that invoke a reaction. The name may well be your own if you are known in your field. If not, choose something distinctive. Avoid bland sets of initials that no one can remember (such as BLTWP) or hugely cumbersome stacks of names like Jones, Duncan, Taylor, Hatstand European Consolidated & Partners. They are not memorable and they imply a lack of clarity on your part.

Every detail counts. Don't skimp on quality of paper or thickness of business cards. Thin business cards are as weak as a limp handshake. Don't have them done at a booth in a railway station! Check the spelling and punctuation really carefully on everything you produce. These days, the world appears to be one large typographical error. Don't be part of it.

When you are describing your business, don't tell people that you haven't really made your mind up about what you want to do, or that you are 'just giving it a go to see what happens'. If you are indecisive about your own concern, you may well unwittingly give the impression that you will be indecisive or unreliable when dealing with your customers. And why would anyone want to do business with someone who has already let you know that they might not be around for long? Customers are much more likely to be loyal to businesses that are reliable and consistent in their own right.

Get connected

These days, computers are an essential element of almost every business. They are not there to ruin your life but to make it easier. Put all your information in your personal organizer and computer, and back up your data regularly to avoid calamity. (Put these back-up reminders in your diary now.) Think carefully about what you want your computer to do for your business, and choose your system accordingly.

- What information might you want to retrieve at some point in the future?
- What might your customers want to know?
- What might you want to know?
- What about your accountant or the dreaded taxman?
- What is the best way of cataloguing your records?
- What is the simplest way of doing all this?

 Make technology work for you
Don't design your system around what the technology can do. Instead, decide what you want from it and design something around those needs. Some careful thought at this stage could save you hours of heartache in the future.

Appoint a good accountant

There are whole books on this one subject, but let's just stick to the basics. You really do need to know how to arrange all your financial affairs from the beginning. You won't want to discover at the end of the year that you have been recording information in the wrong way and that you now have to reorganize everything.

Decide what you need, and organize all your money matters in the easiest possible way. Meeting your accountant once a year should be sufficient, with a few telephone calls every now and then to clarify any details. Keep it simple and think ahead. If you have money problems looming, address them early. Never succumb to the terrible practice of shoving bills in a problem drawer and ignoring them for months – you will create mounting debt and establish a reputation for not paying your suppliers. This is the slippery slope to bankruptcy.

Depending on the nature of your business, here are some of the gritty financial issues that must be addressed right at the beginning.

- Will you be a sole trader or will you register as a company at Companies House?
- Do you need separate bank accounts and, if so, how many?
- How will your tax affairs be arranged?
- Which elements of the business need to be kept financially separate?
- Do you need to rearrange parts of your current personal money habits to adjust to the new set-up?
- Do you need to register for VAT?
- Have you considered national insurance?
- What is the optimum system for paying the lowest amount of tax?

Work out the materials you need

You need to work out precisely what materials you need to run your business. This sounds rather basic but a surprising number of people start their business without really addressing this issue. For example, if you are running a retail outlet, you need to resolve such questions as:

- What stock do I need?
- How much investment is that?
- How quickly can I reorder?
- Do I know where from?
- Do I have the contacts?
- Where will stock be stored?
- Is it safe and secure?
- Is it insured?
- What system will I have for knowing when I am running out?
- Are there legal requirements that I need to take into account?

If you are selling a service, you will need to have as a minimum a clear description of what you are offering cogently written down. This might be in the form of a brochure containing your CV, a client list, some examples of your skills and a list of things that could be of interest to a potential customer.

You will certainly need to state your terms of business. Most businesses start without these and only draw some up after their first debt. But the smart person has them from the beginning to set a precedent and head off financial problems from the off.

Here is a basic checklist of the tools you will need:

- Description of your business ☐
- Your CV ☐
- Your clients ☐
- Examples of what you offer ☐
- Examples of what you have done for others ☐
- Prices ☐
- Terms of business ☐

Network constantly

The main burden of letting people know that you are open for business falls on you. You therefore need to overcome any shyness or reservations you may have about marketing your business.

Have business cards on you all the time, even for social occasions. This is where you may pick up much of your work. Once you start chatting, you'll find that most people are interested in what you do. Without forcing your product or service on them, you will be able always to seem professional by letting them know what you offer and having your contact details to hand.

There's a huge difference between basic marketing and being irritating. Calm, professional marketers state what they do in a clear, charming way. If the reaction of the other person is reasonably positive, they might hand over a card. It's amazing how, months later, the phone rings and a potential new customer says, 'I met you once and now I have a need for what you do...'

'Far and away the best prize that life offers is the chance to work hard at work worth doing.'

Theodore Roosevelt

Summary

Today has been about assuming that you have something to offer, banishing doubts, and working out why anyone should buy what you provide or produce. Being honest with yourself is crucial, because self-deception at this stage will lead to trouble later.

Researching your market thoroughly is important, because someone else may have already used that great idea you had in the pub. Work out how much money you need, and write a simple, realistic plan. Many a launch has been paralysed by constantly reworking the figures, so make clear decisions and move reasonably fast. Invest in a distinctive identity and make sure yours doesn't look the same as anybody else's.

Get connected, because you can't work in a vacuum. Appoint a good accountant – if you mess up the accounts at the beginning, it will cost a lot more to unravel them later. Work out the materials you need, and network constantly without being irritating – people can't use you if they don't know you're there.

Now you must make it happen: inertia ruins many a business.

Fact-check [answers at the back]

1. When starting your own business, what's the right attitude to have?
a) A conviction that I have something to offer ❑
b) Someone else will do all the work ❑
c) It'll never work ❑
d) I'm not much good at what I do ❑

2. How do you set about researching your market?
a) A quick skim should do the trick ❑
b) Ask around, but don't worry about checking too much detail ❑
c) Do it thoroughly, using every source possible ❑
d) Do none and leave it to chance ❑

3. When it comes to money, what should you do?
a) Some rough calculations and then get started ❑
b) Spend months generating lots of spreadsheets ❑
c) Work out precisely how much money you need ❑
d) Calculate the first bit and then do the rest later ❑

4. What's the best way to write a business plan?
a) Write a long, complicated one ❑
b) Get someone else to do it ❑
c) Copy someone else's ❑
d) Write a simple, realistic one ❑

5. When it comes to your company identity, what should you do?
a) Avoid the cost altogether ❑
b) Imitate someone else's ❑
c) Invest in a distinctive one ❑
d) Go for a cheap one ❑

6. When deciding how connected to make your business, what should you do?
a) Get thoroughly connected ❑
b) Go for the bare minimum ❑
c) Assume business will come to you ❑
d) Just use traditional methods ❑

7. What's the right approach to accountants?
a) Avoid them – they're too expensive ❑
b) Use one occasionally ❑
c) Appoint a good one ❑
d) Appoint one without much research ❑

8. What's the best approach to materials?
a) Work it out as you go along ❑
b) Work out everything you need at the beginning ❑
c) Just get the bare minimum to start with ❑
d) Ignore it – something will crop up ❑

9. What should your approach to networking be?

a) Network constantly without being irritating ☐
b) Don't bother – it's not worth it ☐
c) Network with anyone you can get hold of ☐
d) Just do it occasionally ☐

10. What's the right approach to making things happen?

a) Delegate to someone else ☐
b) It'll happen eventually ☐
c) Put it off and hope it all works out ☐
d) It's my business so it's my job to get it done ☐

MONDAY

The right tools for the job

You instinctively know what you'll need in order to start your business, that is to say the tangible items such as systems, stock, premises, materials and so on. With a little thought you can work out your computer software, how often to review the essentials, when to have meetings with your suppliers and associates, and so on. Today we consider the less tangible items: the approaches and disciplines you need in order to motivate yourself to get things done.

A principal theme of this book is that the simpler things are, the better they work. In choosing the right tools for the job, you don't need complicated systems or processes; in fact, they make it less likely that you'll get the job done. Here we look at the elements you need in order to generate some initial business that will get you launched, and to keep it flowing in when you have so much else to do.

Today you'll learn how to:

- design your contact list
- design your business 'hit list'
- keep the numbers manageable
- work out what ratio of meetings generates how much work.

Write out your contact list

'The first step to getting the things you want out of life is this: decide what you want.'

Ben Stein

The contact list is your lifeblood, and should be examined almost every working day. Start the first draft by writing down everyone you know with whom you could possibly do business and with whom you could get in touch. Ideally, it should only have the name of the person, the company and the date you last made contact with them on it.

Don't be tempted to add other information. It will only distract you from the simple matter of picking up the telephone. Everything else is an irrelevant distraction. If you really do feel that you need more information, put it somewhere else. Don't add extraneous detail to the list: it has no bearing on the likelihood of you making the call, organizing a meeting or achieving the thing that needs to be done, but simply blurs your ability to get on with the task in hand.

Every time you speak to someone or meet up with them, write the date down and put their details to the top of the list. This becomes your ready-made recall system. Every time you have a spare moment, look at the very bottom of the list to see who you haven't been in touch with for some time. Having contact details in a different place from your to-do list doesn't work very well because it just gives you another reason for you not to call.

Using the contact list

Having this list means that you can never legitimately claim that you have nothing to do. If you ever do find yourself believing that this is the case (very unlikely when you work on your own, but let's just suspend disbelief for the moment), then you simply go to the bottom of your contact list and call that person for a catch up. If you fix a meeting or do get work as a result of that call, you might give yourself the afternoon off. That's down to you, because only you know whether you deserve it.

After some months have elapsed, draw a 'pester line' at a certain date when you believe it's appropriate to call them again. If you call more than once a month you are probably pestering, but the appropriate frequency will depend on the nature of your business. Every six months is likely to be ideal in a service business where you are involved in one or two projects a year. But if you leave it a year, many of your contacts may have left their company or changed their job description. So work out a frequency of contact that suits the nature of your business, and adjust it if it doesn't seem to be working.

When you call a contact, always tell them when you last spoke or met. They will be impressed by your efficiency. If you have judged the frequency right, the most likely reaction will be, 'Wow, was it that long ago?' This proves that your call is timely, that it is not pestering, and that it represents an appropriate 'keeping in touch' exercise. If they ask you to call back on a certain date, write this date in your personal organizer immediately, and call exactly when they said you should. This level of efficiency confirms that, if you do eventually do some work for them, you will definitely deliver what you say.

Don't overstep the 'pester line'
Keep a constant check on your frequency of contact. If you overdo it, and people start receiving your unwanted solicitations, you'll begin to tarnish your reputation (in other words, you will have overstepped the pester line). You will also be dissipating too much of your time on people who aren't interested in what you have to offer anyway.

How many contacts?

The number of people on your contact list needs constant scrutiny. If there are more than 500 on the list at the outset, you are either fooling yourself or spreading yourself too thinly. It is much better to have a smaller number of viable, genuine prospects than a huge list full of people you don't really know.

On the other hand, if there are fewer than 100 contacts on the list at the outset, your business may well not be viable.

If you were honest with yourself yesterday, then you should have judged this correctly. You need a decent universe against which to apply the normal laws of probability. If you are utterly charmed, it is possible that you could sustain a living on five customers who give you precisely the amount of work that you want exactly when you need it, but it's very unlikely.

In the start-up phase of a service business, you are allowed to have only 50 contacts, but you will definitely need 100 within three months. It's also worth considering whether your founder customers will continue to be long-standing customers and, if so, for how long. You will soon conclude that some will fall away, leaving the onus on you to develop fresh contacts. Be careful to consider this issue early; otherwise, by the time you spot it in the normal run of things, you will already need the new work, and you will be dismayed by the time lag until new work materializes.

Scary but true

If you cannot generate 50 genuine contacts in the start-up phase of a service business, you should probably not be working on your own.

Write out your new business 'hit list'

Another essential tool is the new business 'hit list'. This is a list of everyone you want to get in touch with but have not yet contacted. Generate this hit list once your contact list has taken shape. You need to think carefully and broadly about anyone who could have a bearing on the success of your business. This is not a cynical exercise in exploitation. It is simply casting the net as widely as possible to make the most of the potential contacts that you have. Take your time. This list will not appear as if by magic; you need to rack your brains a bit.

● Don't think only of the one person you know at a company.
● What about their colleagues, bosses and assistants?
● Would approaching several be more advantageous than one only?

- Have you considered friends with interesting jobs?
- Have you reviewed categories where you have related experience?
- Have you scoured the trade press?
- Have you remembered all your past colleagues who have moved on to other things?
- Think back a long way; you may surprise yourself.
- Have you included those who are still at your former places of work?

As a rule of thumb, most of those on this list should be people you don't know, whereas by definition those on the contact list will be known to you, if only initially via a phone conversation.

Put the phone number by every one of them

This may sound pedantic but human nature will dictate that, if the phone number isn't by the name, you have another excuse not to make the call. You will soon realize that, when you work for yourself, making excuses is a form of personal insult. You are effectively saying that you are happy to let yourself get away with it. Well, don't! If the number is by the name, you have no excuse. Now make the calls (see also Thursday's chapter, 'Taming the telephone').

Do everything as soon as you think of it

This is a truism, but it really does work. Think about it. Things either are or they aren't. Have you made the call or not? When you think of something, try to do it immediately. Of course, you cannot literally do everything at once, but what you can do is write down everything that needs doing in a sensible order and work your way through it systematically. This is the way to make things happen. You have a great advantage here: whereas in an office other members of staff keep interrupting you, if you are running your own business, these interruptions are far less frequent so you can get a great deal more done. Ten phone calls in less than an hour? No problem.

TIP Do it when you think of it
'Think, do' is one of the most fundamental principles of the successful businessperson.

Keep the hit list realistic

Constantly review your hit list to see whether you are being realistic. There is no merit in generating a vast list of prospects to call just to make yourself feel good, when in truth you are unlikely to get round to calling them all, or if you might not get through to many of them, let alone get work as a result. Refine your thinking regularly by asking yourself direct questions.

- Where am I likely to have most success?
- Why is a certain approach not working?
- What new approach might work?
- How can I apply one set of skills to another market?
- Have I overlooked an obvious source of business?
- What type of work do I enjoy most?
- Where do I make the best margin?
- Which examples of my previous work are most impressive?

Now start getting the list into some sort of priority order. Put the hottest prospects at the top and revise the order when things change.

As we have seen, it takes less than an hour to make ten phone calls, which of course means that making fewer than ten calls in an hour indicates that you are probably being lazy. You cannot claim that you don't have the time.

Keep the numbers of people on your hit list manageable. If you have any more than 50, you will faze yourself and do nothing, as if you are facing a plate with too much food on it. If you have trouble tackling a list of this size, break it down into manageable chunks that suit you, perhaps into groups of six or ten. Try colour-coding them so that you can distinguish one set from the other.

If your first system doesn't work, simply admit it and invent a new one. Remember, any system is entirely for your own convenience and you don't have to discuss it with anyone else. Just make it work for you.

Invent new ideas for contacting someone

Bright ideas appropriately suggested are always interesting to people, so be vigilant about issues and trends. Pick up on articles in the trade press. Track the movements of people and ideas. It works well when you ring up and say that you've noticed something relevant to them and have a suggestion. It shows that you are on the ball and makes it easier to get work. If you are selling products, keep re-analysing their appeal to your customer base.

● What's 'in' or 'cool' at the moment?
● Do my products fit that mood?
● Can I extend my range?
● What if I run a promotion?
● What if I alter my pricing?
● How about some local marketing?
● Are my marketing materials out of date or looking a bit tired?
● Are there any seasonal events that I should be capitalizing on?

Who should move to my contact list?

The definition of a contact is someone you have met or someone with whom you have had a proper phone conversation. Every time you get through to someone, move them from your hit list to your contact list. At a bare minimum, you will have explained who you are, provided your details and discussed the possibility of work at some point in the future.

Never have someone on your contact list who should be on your new business hit list. They are not a genuine contact until you have spoken to them properly or met them and discussed at least the possibility of working together.

Setting up meetings

In the early days, you need to pull out all the stops to generate some critical mass. That means a lot of meetings and probably a lot of coffee. Try to arrange 20–30 meetings over the first four to six weeks, but keep the meetings short and get to the point. You are a busy person and so are your potential customers. Never book more than four half-hour meetings in a day. You will lose energy and become bored with repeatedly describing what you do. Two meetings a day is ideal. Later on, when you have some paying customers, you can reduce this number and be choosier but, to start with, there is no substitute for putting in the hard work.

The psychology of all this is as follows:

- The amount of business you think you currently have probably isn't as much as you think.
- Something unexpected will happen, so you need contingency income.
- The law of averages will ensure that you will only get a percentage of the business you are aiming for, so you need to work out your 'strike rate'.
- The number of contacts you need in order to fuel your business will be significantly greater than the number of customers or projects that you actually need to run a viable business, so you have to over-compensate, particularly in the start-up phase.

Many people make the classic mistake of arranging meetings and then cancelling them because they are overwhelmed with work. If you think about it, you'll realize that the person you have let down could make a number of assumptions. If you are incredibly lucky, they will be impressed that you are so much in demand, but the more likely reaction is that they now think you are a one-man band who is unable to cope – which means that you certainly won't be able to handle whatever they might have in mind. Goodbye, customer!

Never cancel a new business meeting because you're 'too busy'
Saying, 'I'm sorry, I can't make it because I have too much on' is risky: you may well never get the meeting again, so say yes and just work harder for a brief period.

The telephone is the third essential string to your bow, and we are going to get to grips with it in detail on Thursday. If you have a particular issue with 'cold calling' or any other aspect of phoning people, you might want to read that chapter now. If not, don't worry for the moment. It's not nearly as daunting as you may think. Meanwhile, assuming that you have successfully established your two lists, you have the right tools for the job and you are ready to do business.

Summary

Today you learned how to write up and manage your contact list and new business hit list, to work out who you know, who you don't know and who you want to know. Writing down everyone you want to get in touch with will generate a list of your first potential customers.

Try to do everything when you think of it, otherwise things will drift. 'Think, do' is a good mantra. Constantly review the lists to see whether you are being realistic, and if one area of solicitation isn't working, try another. Keep the numbers manageable, because the big picture can paralyse you. Break it down into bite-size chunks, and keep inventing new ideas for contacting someone.

Every time you get through to someone on your hit list, move them to your contact list. By knowing when you last spoke, you can work out when it might be appropriate to contact them again.

There's no substitute for meeting, talking and suggesting ideas. Never cancel a new business meeting because you are 'too busy': you may never get the meeting back in the diary.

Fact-check [answers at the back]

1. What's the best way to make a contact list?
   a) Keep your contacts in various places such as your phone, computer and notebooks ❏
   b) Don't have one – it gets in the way of getting stuff done ❏
   c) Have it all in the same place with everyone on it who could give you business ❏
   d) Use a spreadsheet ❏

2. What's the best way to write a new business hit list?
   a) Write down details of everyone you want to get in touch with ❏
   b) Write down the top ten and start with them ❏
   c) Just do a few each month ❏
   d) Don't write it down – let leads evolve organically ❏

3. What's the most effective way to make sure you call someone?
   a) Put the phone number by every contact on your list ❏
   b) Have a list of prospects and their numbers programmed into your phone ❏
   c) Have a spreadsheet of names and a separate one for numbers ❏
   d) Choose a name and then look up their number, wherever it is ❏

4. With small tasks, what's the best way to get everything done?
   a) Write a long list ❏
   b) Write a short list ❏
   c) Don't write a list ❏
   d) Do everything when you think of it ❏

5. What's the best way to manage a list of business prospects?
   a) Look at it every day, regardless of whether you are going to take action ❏
   b) Don't look at it much ❏
   c) Constantly review the list to see if you are being realistic ❏
   d) Only look at it when you need more business ❏

6. What's the best way to manage a contact list?
   a) Make it as big as possible ❏
   b) Make it as small as possible ❏
   c) Just pick out the bits you fancy ❏
   d) Keep the numbers manageable ❏

7. What's the best way to secure new business?
   a) Keep telling them the same thing until they get it ❏
   b) Keep inventing new ideas for contacting them ❏
   c) Tell them once and leave them to it ❏
   d) Say you'll call back but then not bother ❏

8. Every time you get through to someone, what should you do with your contact list?
a) Update it straight away ❑
b) Get excited and go to the pub ❑
c) Update it later ❑
d) Tell someone else to update it ❑

9. How many meetings should you aim to fix up in your first four to six weeks?
a) One or two ❑
b) Five to ten ❑
c) 20–30 ❑
d) 50 + ❑

10. You have a new business meeting in three hours and you are very busy. What do you do?
a) Cancel it at the last minute ❑
b) Go anyway ❑
c) Send someone else ❑
d) Cancel it now ❑

SUNDAY

MONDAY

TUESDAY

WEDNESDAY

THURSDAY

FRIDAY

SATURDAY

TUESDAY

Getting the money right

Whatever you do to make a living, and no matter how much you absolutely love it, there is no point in doing it unless you make a sensible amount of money for the effort you put in. So you really owe it to yourself to get the money side of things right. So how exactly do we set about that?

You need to be vigilant about your financial state, but not to the point of micromanagement. Most successful businesses do the right things first and the money follows thereafter.

Today we are going to look at:

- how to concentrate on the money but not become obsessed with it
- weighing up the service vs product distinction
- how to work out the price–quality equation
- not being small-minded about money.

Concentrate on the money

The dreaded money, the filthy lucre. Yes, it's true: from now on, when you discuss money, it will be not in some abstract way based on a remote budget that was agreed by someone you have never met. It will be a highly personal matter.

Now that you are running your own business, every time you discuss money it will all be your personal money, so you need to concentrate hard. It has been said that you don't really appreciate what running your own business means until you have experienced a bad debt, so it's essential that you become comfortable talking about money straight away (but without becoming obsessed by it). If you don't, you will probably agree to produce unspecified amounts of work over unclear time periods. In some instances you might not be paid at all.

Alternatively, you may consistently sell products at margins so low that your business will not be viable. Although this sounds obvious, huge numbers of business people pursue a large volume of sales so that they can brag about the scale of their operation. They crow about turnover, but frequently they are barely making a profit. There is no merit whatsoever in rushing around all year creating things to do when you aren't actually making money. It doesn't make any sense. So address it by keeping a very close eye on your margin, and by constantly questioning *why* you are doing what you are doing.

Weigh up the service versus product distinction

It's difficult to give general guidelines about how to handle money without distinguishing between service- and product-based businesses. If you sell any form of product, then the basic equation of your business will be based on the cost of making or acquiring it in relation to the amount for which you sell it. That's your margin, or, put another way, 'materials with mark-up'. These businesses are almost always less profitable than service businesses that can attribute an acceptable price for an idea or a thing done (unless you are manufacturing a product with such enormous economies of scale that the amount of cash coming in makes the point irrelevant).

Of course, that is a sweeping generalization, but it stands to reason that it is usually easier for a potential customer to attribute a perceived value to a tangible item than it is to an intangible one. In addition, services and ideas often cost nothing other than your time and talent to create. Therefore in theory the price of a service or idea is limitless, whereas that of an item probably has a limit beyond which the market is unlikely to go. Consider this principle in relation to your own business. Ask yourself:

- What level of mark-up will my customers accept?
- What can I do to make what I provide worth more?
- Do I have enough services on offer to increase my average margin?
- Is my pricing appropriate for what I provide?

Sell what you do rather than materials with mark-up

Many other things can make an enormous difference to your profitability. Your talents theoretically have a limitless price.

That means that, within certain sensible parameters, you can charge what you want. Materials are finite and have an approximate known price, so a competitor can often undercut you and so decrease your margin. The smartest businesses do not sell materials or any fixed-price service. They sell experience and ideas. This is not a way to rip off customers – quite the opposite, in fact.

The answer to the question of how much you can charge is fascinating. Some potential customers will not have the foresight to estimate (or, in their eyes, speculate wildly) what they might gain by engaging your services. In which case, they won't answer the question or will not be prepared to say that the answer might be quite a large figure. This means either that they are not a genuine potential customer or that they will be a penny-pinching bad one, which means that you should not be pursuing their business anyway.

An enlightened potential customer will rapidly be able to put a likely figure on what they stand to gain (or not lose) from your involvement, and they will be big enough to tell you the true amount. Once you get into honest conversations of this type, you can forge a direct link between your price and the customer benefit. After a number of similar conversations, you may well have enough evidence and confidence to double your prices.

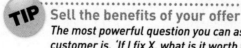

TIP Sell the benefits of your offer
The most powerful question you can ask a client or customer is, 'If I fix X, what is it worth to your business?'

The price–quality equation

If you cost a lot, you must be good
What do you deduce about two products of similar type, one of which costs £2,000 and the other £200? The more expensive one is probably better made and so of higher quality. It may well have a cachet or brand value to which potential buyers aspire. There is nothing wrong with it being more expensive, assuming that there are people who appreciate those qualities and are prepared to pay for it. No matter how disparaging one chooses

to be about products and services that are 'expensive', one is eventually forced to admit that, one way or another, there must be a demand for them or they would not remain on the market.

In which case, what would you deduce about two people offering a service, one of whom commands a fee of £2,000 a day and the other £200? The more expensive person is likely to be more experienced and therefore of higher quality. This is self-fulfilling because, if they are not, then in a fairly short time they will not generate any repeat business and will soon have to reduce their prices or fail as an enterprise. It may be something of a rhetorical question, but which of these two people would you rather be? If you think it through carefully, you will pretty much always look enviously upon someone who is successful in a particular field and come to the following conclusion:

If they cost a lot, they must be good
This is, of course, the reaction that you should aim to invoke in your customers and competitors. Your central maxim should be: charge a premium price and do a great job.

Charge a premium price and do a great job
Clearly there has to be an appropriate balance between price and delivery but, in the main, you should always place the maximum possible value on what you have to offer.

The benefits of working alone

Ever heard of 'high-maintenance' members of staff? One of the most time-consuming issues in any business is other people. No one is suggesting that you become a hermit, and it may well be that your business genuinely cannot function without a workforce. However, if you are working for yourself, you do at least have the option to consider structuring a business that minimizes the effect others can have on your fortunes. So you owe it to yourself to consider whether there is any possibility that you *could* run your business without anyone else. If there is any chance that you might, it is a strongly recommended option. Why? Because when you are on your own you:

- make clearer decisions
- make faster decisions
- do business in your own unique style

- avoid having to deal with politics
- do not have to feel guilty about relationships with colleagues
- can experience a truly direct link between effort and reward.

Aim for repeat business

You should aim for 50 per cent repeat business within three years. If this aim frightens you, there's something wrong with your ambitions. Do you expect your customers to be pleased with the work you do? If the answer is yes, which it certainly should be, then you should expect further work in due course. If you are selling products, there is still a service element to what you do, so your objective must be to have your customers coming back. Even taking account of the random availability of projects, seasonal factors and the cyclical nature of certain markets, you should always aspire to getting more business from at least half your existing customers.

45

You should also track satisfied customers when they move house, move to new jobs or have any other change of circumstances. Whatever has happened, they will be confronted by a whole new set of issues, many of which you may well be able to address. In a service business in particular, it is important to go and have a coffee with people when they move. It is flattering for them, it gives you a flavour of their new set-up and there is always something new to discuss.

Of course, aiming for 50 per cent could be criticized as banal. Who in their right mind would aim for a percentage? It is merely a figure that will fluctuate anyway, depending on the size and shape of the other elements in your business. Fair enough. What should make sense, though, are the parameters above and below which repeat purchase levels should not rise or fall. If you have 100 per cent repeat business, then the corollary is that you have no new business. This is not good. If you have no repeat business, then you would certainly be worried about the quality and value of what you produce and the long-term prospects for your business, if only judged by word-of-mouth recommendation and customer satisfaction. And if you had a fantastic run of new business, then you would not mind at all if your repeat percentage fell. So perhaps we should conclude that the percentage should be no lower than 30 per cent and no higher than 70 per cent in any given year.

'We have no money so we will have to think.'

Lord Rutherford

Don't be small-minded about money

Think big. Now that you will probably have to type all your own invoices and do your own VAT return, don't waste time with bits and pieces that don't get you anywhere. When quoting and invoicing, stick to units of hundreds or thousands of pounds. It is difficult to generalize here, but the basic rule is not to dither about with small fractions that don't really add to your profit, but which infuriate you when doing the books. Keep it simple and round the figures up or down (preferably up) in order to get the job done quickly and efficiently. In some instances you may lose a little on price, and in others you may gain a little, but you will save hours of fiddling about with pounds and pence.

This is an extension of the "successful people buy in bulk" principle, and it applies to anyone who works on their own. In a service business, be generous and broad-minded. Buy the client lunch and pay for your own travel. Don't forget that your accountant can make allowances for all sorts of things and tidy up all the details at the end of the year. That's what you pay them for.

Successful business people buy in bulk

This is so that they don't have to waste time perpetually buying individual small units of a given item. This applies to pretty much everything: paper, paper clips, printer cartridges, stamps, envelopes – that rather irritating list of stuff which has to be bought but doesn't really seem to have a bearing on anything. No matter what your business, don't be petty about these expenses. If at all possible, never charge them to the customer but, if appropriate, build a suitable margin into your prices to allow for any extra services that you would normally wish to offer them.

Considering requests for free or 'win only' work

'Share in our success or failure' was one of the worst traits of the dot.com boom of the late 1990s. This is a euphemism for 'I won't pay for anything unless things have gone really well and I decide that I can afford it.' The main rule here is never to give anything away for free unless you have an overwhelming reason for doing so. When people ask why you won't do speculative work, the best answer is, 'Because I don't need to.' There really is no response to that.

Although there is usually no reason to give your time away for free, you do of course reserve the right to charge less or provide free work if you deem it appropriate. You should try not to, but you are the best judge of any given state of affairs, and the joy of running your own business is that you don't have to discuss your decision with anyone else.

Here are some possible reasons why you *might* want to provide something free or at a reduced price:

- It will lead to repeat business.
- It will lead to new business.
- It's part of a much bigger deal.
- It's a highly valued customer.
- Because you can.

One other way of thinking about offering free work is to donate your time and know-how to a worthy cause. If you have had a really good year, why not offer to work free for a charity for a limited period? Your expertise may well be worth significantly more than any donation you might ordinarily make, and skills are often more useful than cash. No money needs to change hands and you can add their name to your client list and use it as part of your sales patter.

Summary

Today we looked at the money side of your business and how to generate a healthy margin. You learned that being obsessed with money and wandering round with a spreadsheet all day are not how to get the business working. Ask yourself whether you are offering a service, a product or both, and try to sell what you do, not materials with mark-up. Products have price points that are easier for the customer to guess, whereas services can be priceless. Can you offer something that relies purely on your skill or experience?

Consider the price–quality equation: if you cost a lot, you must be good. People like to pay for high-quality goods and services, so don't sell yourself cheap. If you can earn a living and stay sane on your own, you can avoid the most time-consuming issue: other people. Aim for 50 per cent repeat business within three years, and aspire to the high standards that generate it. Don't be small-minded about money: speculate and you'll accumulate. Don't go bust by spending your first year behaving like a charity, but be canny about requests for free or 'win only' work.

Fact-check [answers at the back]

1. In your business, what should be your attitude to money?
   a) Check it all the time ❏
   b) Never check it ❏
   c) Assume it'll work out fine ❏
   d) Concentrate on it, but don't become obsessed with it ❏

2. When choosing whether to provide services or products, what's the best thing to do?
   a) Work out if you can make a better margin by providing a service ❏
   b) Make products if at all possible ❏
   c) Ignore the whole thing – it's a false distinction ❏
   d) Buy stuff in and put a whopping mark-up on it ❏

3. When deciding how to charge for a service, what's the best thing to do?
   a) Copy someone else's pricing ❏
   b) Work out how to have a healthy margin ❏
   c) Charge it at cost to you ❏
   d) Add a modest few percent mark-up ❏

4. Which of these ideas should you ignore when starting a business?
   a) Consider doing without offices and work from home ❏
   b) Try operating without a business partner ❏
   c) Pay yourself less for a while ❏
   d) Delegate everything and leave it to chance ❏

5. What's the most time-consuming issue in a start-up?
   a) Dealing with staff ❏
   b) Doing the books ❏
   c) Dealing with suppliers ❏
   d) Dealing with customers ❏

6. What's the best way to make money?
   a) Sell materials with a mark-up ❏
   b) Sell what you do ❏
   c) Make a margin on what someone else does ❏
   d) Do a mixture ❏

7. What's the right attitude to pricing?
   a) If you cost a lot, you must be expensive ❏
   b) If you are cheap, then so is the product or service ❏
   c) If you cost a lot, you must be good ❏
   d) If you are cheap, then it's good value ❏

8. What's an ideal level of repeat business within three years?
   a) 10% ❏
   b) 20% ❏
   c) 50% ❏
   d) 100% ❏

9. What's the right attitude to money?
a) Save every penny – you never know when you'll need it ❏
b) Keep it tight – times are hard ❏
c) Splash it around – even if you're in debt ❏
d) Be generous – the rewards will come ❏

10. You are asked to do something for free. What's the correct approach?
a) Be canny about it – treat each case as it comes ❏
b) No way – I can't afford it ❏
c) Yes – any time you like ❏
d) You've got a cheek to ask ❏

SUNDAY

MONDAY

TUESDAY

WEDNESDAY

THURSDAY

FRIDAY

SATURDAY

WEDNESDAY

Communicating effectively

Communication must surely be one of the most complicated issues in life, let alone in a business context. Where would we be without it? Humans cannot exist without it. Almost everything we do involves the need for it. And yet often we really aren't very good at it. So let's have a look at some of the methods at our disposal and work out how best to use them.

Today we are going to look at:

- choosing the right communication method
- becoming adept at describing what you do in 30 seconds
- introducing some humanity into your CV
- why it's important to meet plenty of people and stay open-minded
- the importance of paying attention to customers and asking them what they want.

Choose the right communication method

'Never be afraid to tell the world who you are.'

Anon.

Methods of communicating are constantly changing. Until relatively recently you could only really talk to someone in person, telephone them or write a letter. That was about it. You might have faxed someone or sent a courier to speed things up a bit. Then came the Internet and mobile telephony, and the whole scene changed. We now require a much broader set of communication skills, and we need to put a lot more thought into deciding which is the appropriate method for any particular situation.

We can put these options into some sort of hierarchy. Here is a rank order of possible communication methods, based on (a) the likelihood of you being correctly understood and (b) probable sales success as a result:

1 Talking face to face
2 Telephone conversation
3 Letter
4 Email

With regard to effectiveness, option number one must beat all the rest by 100 to 1. If at all possible, always conduct your important business face to face. However, this is not an excuse for endorsing a 'meetings culture' in which legions of earnest businesspeople sit in meetings all day without really knowing why: quite the opposite, in fact. It is perfectly possible to conduct meetings in a brisk, polite way that acknowledges the fact that most people are busy. Come in, get to the point, agree what is to be done, and get out. Half an hour is the ideal length for a business meeting.

Having a good telephone conversation can also be highly productive, but there's a huge difference between having one

with someone you have not met in person and someone you can picture. Everything is easier if you have met and so, if it is important, make sure that you do indeed meet.

Letter writing is next down the list, but a very long way behind. In the direct marketing industry, the average response rate to letters is around 2 per cent. It wouldn't be much use if you only got through to two out of every 100 of your prospects, so letters have to serve a very distinct purpose.

Finally, we come to the dreaded email. In many respects, this method has completely revolutionized our lives. Certainly, many people running their own business could not succeed without it because of its fantastic ability to deliver things quickly and its power to enable them to stay in touch. However, as a high-quality communication method, email leaves a lot to be desired. Response levels to mass emailings are now as low as old-fashioned direct mail – around 2 per cent. Emailing has other drawbacks too:

- Anything you send can be ignored.
- The presentation style is often up to the recipient, not you.
- Most messages are not checked, and any errors can make you look unprofessional.
- People you don't know about are sometimes blind-copied on the original for political purposes that you know nothing about.
- Your original message or reply is often forwarded to someone you know nothing about.

Suffice it to say that any communication method that has these pitfalls needs to be treated with extreme caution.

Describe what you do in less than 30 seconds

Potential customers may be interested in what you do for a maximum of one minute. This is true at an interview, a drinks party, in the pub, at the squash club – anywhere, in fact. After that, they become bored. So you need to get your act together and come across in a lucid, enthusiastic way.

Start by writing down what you do in no more than three sentences. Now read it out loud. Does it sound daft? If so, rewrite it. Try again. Does it sound like a cliché? Does it sound like all the other waffle you read in corporate brochures or hear from politicians on the television? If so, change it. Make it fun and engaging. Do it with some pride and a lot of energy. Excellent: now you can use it for face-to-face conversations, telephone calls and all your written work. Also bear in mind that this 'pitch' should evolve constantly to keep pace with the manner in which your business develops.

On the other hand, don't be afraid to improvise on the spot. Life's a mess. Make it up as you go along! One of the joys of running your own business is that you can change the rules any time you like – several times a day in fact, if you are feeling particularly mischievous. There's nothing more boring than someone who repeats the company mantra in a soulless manner, so go with the flow a bit. If you spot an opportunity, try out a sales angle. If you have a random thought, say it. If you want to discuss an idea without necessarily proposing it, then do so. It's vibrant and fun.

Introduce humanity into your CV

We've all seen the type of thing: 'Relentlessly successful, moved from A to B to C, married with two children, enjoys theatre and music.'

That's the gist of the average CV. What can we deduce about this individual? Are they extremely reliable or just boring? The best that we can guess is that this is a fairly steady individual. Let's compare them with the next one.

'Gained experience doing X, transferred skills to different industry Y, broke away and set up on own doing Z, plays in a rock band, flies birds of prey at the weekends, amateur artist and occasional cartoonist.'

Who would you prefer to have a drink with? Who would you rather do business with? You get the idea. If you introduce some humanity into your business life, interesting things start to happen.

Firstly, you get to know your customers so much better, not because you are asking inane questions such as 'Did you have a good weekend?' but because you really get to know what they are up to. In most cases people do some very interesting and enterprising things that they never mention unless you ask. Secondly, if you work in the type of business where it is appropriate to overlap your work and social life, the whole thing becomes a pleasure instead of a chore. Thirdly, smart customers deduce very quickly that if you are enterprising in your spare time, then you probably are in your working time as well.

Meet lots of people and stay open-minded

You need to stay open-minded. Bear in mind that every meeting you have involves a judgement of character as well as an assessment of someone's technical skills. The more people you communicate with, the more experience you will have of working out whether you'll get on well with them, and whether they will be relevant to your aspirations for your business. Once you have met, you need to keep a close eye on what happens next. Try asking yourself these questions:

- Did they send through the thing that they said they would in the meeting?
- Did they call in two weeks' time as they promised?
- Did they give my details to their colleague as we agreed?
- Did they consider my proposal and give me a response?

If the answer to any of these is yes, you may be on to a decent working relationship. If the answer is mainly no, you need to consider carefully whether the person is a time waster or someone who usually fails to do what they say they will. If this proves to be the case, they will not be fulfilling to do business with, and, if they are an associate of any kind, be aware that their poor approach will also reflect badly on you.

Once you've met a lot of people, you can refine your approach into some proper networking. This is not a cynical process whereby you screw every last piece of benefit from people and give them nothing back. You keep in touch, help them out, suggest things and, ideally, do business together. Everyone wins.

Take your customers to lunch

It could be lunch. It could be breakfast, dinner, the races, or even just a beer. The details don't matter. The thing is that social surroundings promote a totally different mood from those of meeting rooms, many of which appear to be designed precisely to *reduce* the chances of meetings being enjoyable. Suggesting a social get-together is a constructive, magnanimous thing to do. What does it say about you? It says that:

● you are open-minded
● you are interested in other aspects of your customers than just their money
● you can afford it.

You'll be engineering a situation in which you can show your generosity (by insisting on paying), your interest in them, and quite possibly the degree to which you are on the ball with your suggestions of places to go and things to do.

What do you talk about when you meet up? You'll do a bit of business, certainly, but mainly, just ask short, open-ended questions and then shut up. You'll be amazed at what comes up. People will talk when they are put at ease. They will talk about their families and relationships, their concerns, their feelings about their job, sport, hobbies, and current affairs – pretty much anything. Of course there are some bores in the world, but in the main there are interesting things to learn and discuss. The more ideas you have, the smarter you will appear, not because you are faking it but because it will be true. It's all part of honing good communication skills.

Rewrite your marketing materials

Assuming that you do succeed in creating a dynamic environment for your business, things will probably change quite rapidly and so should the manner in which you describe what you do. The chances are that your marketing materials will become obsolete pretty quickly, so update them. It doesn't have to be an expensive exercise if you stick to the basics and concentrate on the elements that work well in your market.

Get out all the stuff that you have done and spread it out on a large table. Ask yourself some questions:

- What do I think of the materials?
- Do they accurately represent what I do these days?
- Which bits worked and which didn't?
- What can I learn from that?
- Do I use some elements more than others?
- Has the emphasis of my business changed?
- Is there any point in producing something new?

Design a clever offer for customers

Don't be one of those businesses that sends out one launch mailing and then sits back thinking that they have 'done marketing'. The market is changing all the time. People come and go. Products and tastes change. You can never conclusively prove that something that didn't work before won't work now. So consider the merits of sending out a new offer to your customers and ask yourself:

- What would I say?
- If I have done it before, did I learn anything?
- Who would I send it to – existing customers for repeat purchase or new potential customers?
- If so, where will I get their details?

Tell customers what you can do for them

How many businesses plough on churning out the same old stuff, assuming that what they provide is what their customers want? Most people don't like change, unless someone else does all the work and makes it a pleasure. Then they can opt in or out on their own whim and in their own time. Unfortunately, when you run your own business, that someone is you. It is your job to stay very close to your customers and the markets in which you operate.

When you have some new ideas that you want to test, or even if you have none at all (hopefully not, otherwise you may well be lacking the entrepreneurial spirit shown by most people who want to start their own business), talk to your customers. People love nifty ideas, especially when they are well timed. Ask them:

● **What else could I do for you?**
   – Did you realize that what I do for you is only a fraction of what I do for some of my other customers?
   – How much does what I do make a difference to your business?
   – What are the main things preoccupying you at the moment?
   – Would you like me to investigate something new for you?
   – Are you dissatisfied with any suppliers who provide similar services to me?
   – Do you know any other potential customers who might want to use my services?
● **What could I do better?**

By now you will know that, when you ask such open-ended questions, it's your job to shut up and pay attention. The new selling opportunities are always lurking in the answers given. Let them talk. In many instances, your customers will invent new work for you on the spot. Occasionally, drop in new ideas or offer to develop a thought into a proposal.

TIP

Suggest a new idea to your customers
Offer to do a little development work on a subject and call the customer in a week's time to see whether it's worth proceeding.

Summary

Today you learned the importance of communicating effectively with customers, whether that is face to face or by phone, email or letter. You can now describe what you do in less than 30 seconds – because if you can't, why should anyone else try to understand it – while being prepared to improvise and to ask yourself, if a potential customer has a need, whether you can fill it.

Introduce some humanity into your CV to give people a flavour of what you'd be like to work with. People give business to people they like, so make sure that you're a pleasure to be around. Go out and meet people, stay open-minded and don't close off opportunities before they can develop.

Take your customers to lunch and insist on paying because, when the boundaries between business and social life blur, you are on to something. Keep your marketing materials up to date, design a clever offer to send to customers and ask them what else you might do for them – you never know, you may be able to help them in other ways than currently.

Fact-check [answers at the back]

1. When communicating with customers and prospects, what should you do?
   a) Think carefully about the right method ❏
   b) Try everything and see what happens ❏
   c) Try one method and hope for the best ❏
   d) Copy your competitors ❏

2. How long should you take to describe what you do?
   a) Less than five minutes ❏
   b) Less than three minutes ❏
   c) Less than a minute ❏
   d) Less than 30 seconds ❏

3. How should you go about describing your business?
   a) Make it up as you go along ❏
   b) Be prepared to improvise ❏
   c) Stick to a set speech and don't deviate ❏
   d) Freeze and say nothing ❏

4. What should you do when drawing up your CV?
   a) Keep it quite formal ❏
   b) Pretend you are a large corporation ❏
   c) Introduce some humanity into it ❏
   d) Mimic that of a competitor ❏

5. When it comes down to it, who do people usually do business with?
   a) People they like ❏
   b) People they don't like ❏
   c) People they have no opinion about ❏
   d) People like them ❏

6. When starting a business, what's the best way to win customers?
   a) Meet lots of people and weigh them up carefully ❏
   b) Meet lots of people and stay open-minded ❏
   c) Pick people off systematically in a carefully rehearsed move ❏
   d) Stay in the office and let them come to you ❏

7. When you have secured a regular customer, what's the right approach?
   a) Milk them for all they are worth ❏
   b) Give them a small discount ❏
   c) Do nothing ❏
   d) Take them to lunch and insist on paying ❏

8. If your marketing isn't working, what should you do?
   a) Rewrite your marketing materials ❏
   b) Abandon all marketing efforts ❏
   c) Do the 'more of the same' approach ❏
   d) Get someone else to do it ❏

9. What should you do to become even more profitable?
   a) Offer a discount to your customers ❏
   b) Design a clever offer to send to your customers ❏
   c) Spend money on trying to get more customers ❏
   d) Do nothing and leave it alone ❏

10. What's the best way to expand your business?

a) Invent a new product ❏

b) Ask your customers what else you could do for them ❏

c) Open a new outlet as fast as possible ❏

d) Carry on – it's business as usual ❏

SUNDAY
MONDAY
TUESDAY
WEDNESDAY
THURSDAY
FRIDAY
SATURDAY

THURSDAY

Taming the telephone

The phone can be either a two-way machine that is a great asset to your business or an object that invokes considerable fear. Many people hate what they describe as 'cold calling'. If you are one of them, and particularly if you are in a service business, you need to address this issue urgently and befriend your phone. Once you get the hang of it, it's really not as bad as you think.

Anyone starting their own business needs to confront certain things with regard to the telephone. Start by reading this chapter and try to apply some of the suggestions. Whatever you do, don't reject the idea before you have a go – it is not nearly as onerous as many would have you believe.

Today we are going to look at ways to:

- overcome fears and prejudices about 'cold calling'
- understand the relationship between the number of calls and the eventual amount of work
- prepare your selling angles
- have a system for noting your calls.

Don't call it 'cold calling'

Who said cold calling was cold? Rarely has an activity been so badly named. Calling someone on the phone is usually a very pleasant thing to do. It is far better to view the whole process as just calling someone for a chat. The fact that you have never met has nothing to do with it. If you are charming and have something interesting to say, then it will be a pleasure for both sides.

There are lots of ways to get the conversation started and overcome the initial hurdles. One way to do this is to consider all the worst things that could possibly happen if things don't go as well as you hoped. Here are some examples:

● **They say they are not interested in what you do.**
So what? This is very valuable information. Many people spend weeks, months, years even, pursuing someone who simply isn't interested in what they have to offer, and never will be. This could be an individual or a company whose culture doesn't suit yours, and vice versa. Take it on the chin and move on.

● **They refuse to take your call.**
This is most interesting. If someone spends the bulk of their time hiding behind a barrage of secretaries and assistants,

you can deduce one of two things about them. Either they may be genuinely busy, or they enjoy creating the impression that they are busy. If it is the former, then it doesn't mean that they are not interested in what you do. Either keep trying or use a different method of getting in touch that suits their style better.

● **They are rude or dismissive.**
This is a bit unpleasant but no less helpful than either of the above. Rude people may well occupy influential positions for intermittent periods, but nobody enjoys working with them and, over time, the system spits them out. If you work on your own, there is absolutely no point in dealing with people of this type. They ruin your life and they do not deserve your contribution. Avoid them at all costs.

Use the phone to market yourself

Admit that the phone will never ring unless you market yourself. Many people who set up on their own make the mistake of thinking that the phone will ring and provide them with work in the same way that it did when they were employed in a company. It doesn't. In fact, on some days it doesn't ring at all. One or two extremely blessed individuals come out of corporate life and seem to have a charmed flow of ready-made work without appearing to have to market themselves. But one thing is for sure: it never lasts. In year two or three, these people are left adrift as that source of business fades.

Besides, you may not even have a contact base from a former life, so you need to market from the outset, to a fairly broad audience. The first stepping stone in this process is admitting that the phone is unlikely to ring unless you make it. In other words, you need to create the momentum that makes people want to call you back, whether that is today or at some point in the future when they have a need for your product or service. This is simple logic. If you don't ask the girl out, she won't even know you are interested. If you don't call and express an interest, then potential customers won't consider you.

If you make 100 calls, you'll get 40 meetings and 3 jobs

The precise figures may vary, depending on the nature of your business, but the essence of the equation never does. Take a moment to think about this. It stands to reason that you must generate a critical mass of interest in what you have to offer. The mathematics of it has nothing to do with the quality of you, your product or service or your customer base. If you jot down all the possible reasons why someone does *not* want to do business with you this week, you will soon see how circumstances are more likely to stop work happening than to start it.

Remember: 100 calls = 40 meetings = 3 jobs

This is why people talk about 'the pipeline' in a new business context. In truth, it is more helpful to see it as a funnel or hopper. The work appears to come sequentially in a linear way, but actually it only appears to be that way because, at any given moment, you have many contacts and proposals which, in all probability, will generate work at some point, but not necessarily now. It never happens all at once, and that is precisely why you need a regular flow of people who just might be interested in your offer in any given week or month.

Prepare your selling angles

'Sell the crunch not the apple.'

Anon.

Now let's get down to the business of what you are actually going to say on the phone. You've done the hard part: you've sat down with a list of people to call, researched all their numbers and you've dialled. So what exactly are you going to say? You need to consider some selling angles:

- Who am I?
- What do I do?

- Why am I calling?
- What do I (or my business) offer?
- What has it got to do with them?
- What do I want to happen next?
- What happens if they are not there and someone else answers?

You need to work through all these possibilities before you call. Don't dial and then panic. If you have considered all the angles beforehand, you won't be caught on the hop.

 Never leave a message
If you do, you immediately cede control of the contact to the other person. This means that, the moment you call again, you are pestering.

Don't use jargon to disguise what you do

Once you've got through to the person you want to speak to, stay calm. Remember that waffle and jargon are the last preserve of corporate behemoths such as lawyers. We all know that obscure phraseology is designed to confuse people so that it seems as though they need the services offered (and can be charged more). When you run your own business, the opposite is true: if the person at the other end can't grasp what you do in one sentence, they won't bother to listen to the rest, so cut out the waffle and get straight to the point.

Use clear, simple expressions to explain what you do and why you would like to do business with them. Don't be vague about what you do – let them grasp it quickly and move the conversation on to the area that matters to you.

If you find this difficult, try these techniques:

- Pretend that you're explaining it to your mother.
- Phrase it as though you were talking to your mate in the pub.
- Write it down and eliminate anything that sounds silly.
- Say it out loud and ask yourself whether you sound daft.

- Tape record it, listen back, and decide whether you would welcome such a phone call.
- Practise saying it in front of the mirror.

Finally, try it on the phone, and then debrief yourself as to whether you sounded sensible. If you're not happy with your message for any reason, draw up a new version.

Make sure you do all this *before* you call.

Tell them you're available

There is a tendency in modern business to want to create the impression that you are always frantically busy. This is completely inappropriate for someone who runs their own business. You need to strike the right balance. For a start, people soon detect whether you always *claim* to be very busy, and they probably won't believe that's always true. Secondly, if you really are so incredibly busy, how will you fit in the proposed work for them? Think about it; you need to convey the impression that you would like their business, but that it's not essential that you have it today. Desperation does not work; confidence and calmness do.

Another side effect of always appearing to be frantically busy is that there is a distinct possibility that you will convey the impression that you are disorganized as well. This is a poor signal to be sending out. There is a good balance to be found in always making yourself available for potential business, but on your own terms and in your own time (within reason). Obviously, you don't wish to come across as indifferent, but you should reserve the right to pace the flow of any new business advances to make sure that you deliver appropriately for your existing customers, because they pay the bills. So when you are talking on the phone, make it clear that you are available to do the necessary work.

Try selling the opposite of everyone else

It is also very trendy at the moment to promote yourself or your business as specialists. Somehow, people think it is more reassuring if they have a 'specialism'. While there is some evidence that certain specialists are able to charge more for their services, business people can usually fix a whole range of issues, so it's important to think broadly. This is very likely to increase your opportunities, your income and the breadth of your work. This in turn will introduce greater variety to your work.

Of course, this suggestion presupposes that you are indeed capable of doing more than one type of thing. In theory it is possible that you genuinely cannot, but most people have more than one talent, and those who are capable of working on their own are certainly at the more enterprising end of the spectrum, so they are usually used to fixing a range of problems. Give it some thought. Try portraying yourself as a generalist, not a specialist. You may well get more work, and you will in all probability enjoy yourself more by venturing into new areas that you haven't tried before.

Tell them it's simple (because you are experienced)

Saying that something is really complicated does not inspire confidence and is as dismaying as a plumber staring at your boiler and declaring, 'We'll never get the parts for this.' By all means appear thoughtful and reflective, but then tell the customer that you have dealt with a similar issue before and that you know what to do – particularly if this is the first time you have spoken on the phone.

Offer to solve their issue quickly

Customers often commission work not because they cannot do it themselves but because they don't have time. So it is often appropriate to tell them that they could certainly do the work themselves, but would it help if you took it off their 'things to do' list for a certain price? At this point, speed and convenience may become more relevant than your precise skill set.

Doing something quickly doesn't mean that the work is bad quality or bad value; it may in fact be precisely what the customer wants. As the old story goes, if a portrait costs

£10,000, the painter is charging that for a lifetime's experience, regardless of whether he or she does the job in a day or a month. An experienced mechanic might diagnose and cure a problem in half an hour. An amateur might take all day, and may even do a poorer job of fixing it. The fast solution may thus actually be the higher-quality one, assuming that the person doing the job knows exactly what they are doing.

This approach is also a pleasant counterpoint to suppliers who want to make a job last longer so that they can charge more. Don't string out a job in order to charge a higher price but offer to fix something quickly, based on the assumption that you are experienced enough to know what you are doing and organized enough to schedule it in efficiently and get on with it.

Sell your value, not your time
The speed with which you can do something has absolutely no bearing on the value.

Tell them who else you work for

People love case histories and, when you catch them on the phone, they don't usually have much time. So they want easy anchor points with which to base their purchasing decision, just like references on a CV. They want to know the answers to these questions:

● Who else have you worked for?
● What did you do for them?
● Can I have some examples?

You need to anticipate these requests, and after a short while you should be able to rattle these off effortlessly, even in your early days when you may actually be using examples from your previous corporate life. You do not always have to refer to something directly related to the task in hand, but you should become adept at drawing on examples and making links between issues.

Customers don't always want people with direct experience of their field. Very often, people in particular businesses have become too close to the issues that they encounter every day. So don't be sheepish about your skills – just think broadly and suggest how your strengths could benefit the issue being discussed.

Talk about price and timing

Don't start discounting on the phone, before you've even met. State your rates clearly and without embarrassment. If the customer balks at the cost, say that you can discuss it when you meet, and when you have better understood the nature of the possible work. Anyone who works on their own has examples of potential clients who have exclaimed 'How much?' only to come back later having had a poor experience elsewhere with a cheaper alternative.

There are really only three variables at stake when a customer is considering whether to make a purchase: quality, price and timing. Put simply, the three questions are:

1 Will it do the job?
2 How much will it cost?
3 When can I have it?

When you are negotiating, it's essential to remember that you can always offer some flexibility on any two of these three variables but never on all three. For example, you may be able to reduce the price if you are given a longer time. You may be able to do the work more quickly if you can charge more. While no one will ever admit to wanting low quality, things can be short-circuited.

A good way to remember this negotiating stance is to try starting every sentence with the word 'if'. This ensures that you interrelate all the variables so that you never give all three away and end up in a compromised position. For example, say, 'If I have to deliver it by Friday, the price will have to increase' or, 'If you need the price to be lower, I'll need longer to do the job.'

Have a system for noting your calls

As discussed on Monday, it's vital to keep a full list of all your contacts and have a system for contacting them. Keep your list up to date and choose an appropriate contact frequency for your business that does not represent pestering. By all means note some detail about what was said if you think you might forget, but don't clutter up the list with irrelevant information that might impede your next call. Staying organized in this area says volumes about your reliability and efficiency.

- The appropriate timing of your call says that you are diligent but not desperate or aggressive.
- The fact that you know when you last spoke shows that you are on the ball.
- The fact that you did indeed call back when you said you would means that you are thoroughly organized and are therefore likely to be similarly efficient when doing a job for them.
- If you have a new idea, or have noted a development in their business circumstances to which you can refer, that's even better.

Be natural and human

It's important to remember one final point when you are talking with someone for the first time on the phone: to be natural and remain true to your character. Keep your pride. Don't apologize for calling, and don't do down what you have to offer. There is every chance that they will find your call helpful and interesting. You'll never know unless you ask.

Remember the central principle of running your own business: only do business with people you like. If they don't want to use you, it doesn't really matter. If they won't talk to you, it doesn't matter. Not everybody works with everyone else, and you will derive far more job satisfaction from working with people whose company you enjoy and who genuinely appreciate your contribution.

All you need is enough work to keep you stimulated and solvent. No adverse response is personal – it's just business – so if it's not happening with a particular prospect, let it go and keep your self-esteem intact. On the other hand, you will be jubilant when you have completed a successful call that has given you work. Then you will definitely know that you have tamed the telephone.

Summary

Today you learned not to call it 'cold calling': you might think it's cold but the other person might not. Admit that the phone will never ring unless you market yourself; you won't get any business unless you put in the effort. Prepare your selling angles and become adept at describing what you do in less than 30 seconds. If you waffle or use jargon, they won't get it. Tell them you're available, because no one wants to wait if they need something.

Think broadly when describing your offer on the phone. Tell them that their issue is simple (because you are experienced) and offer to solve it quickly – remember, no one wants to wait if they need something. Be ready with examples of other customers for whom you work. If you did it for someone else, you can do it for them.

Don't start discounting before you've even met. A customer might be perfectly happy with the full price. Use a call-logging system and call again when appropriate. Finally, be as natural and human as you can. Don't go into business mode on the phone – just be your normal self.

Fact-check [answers at the back]

1. What do you call phoning someone to ask if they will give you some business?
a) Out of the question – I won't do it ☐
b) A scary conversation ☐
c) Cold calling ☐
d) A perfectly ordinary means of discussing business ☐

2. When starting up, what attitude to the phone should you have?
a) It will never ring unless I market myself ☐
b) It'll ring regardless of what I do ☐
c) It might ring – we'll see who's around to answer ☐
d) I'll use other channels like the web ☐

3. How many calls do you need to make to get 40 meetings?
a) 200 ☐
b) 100 ☐
c) 50 ☐
d) 5 ☐

4. How many jobs will come from 40 meetings?
a) 1 ☐
b) 3 ☐
c) 20 ☐
d) 30 ☐

5. What's the best way to sell on the phone?
a) Choose a line and stick to it ☐
b) Make it up as you go along ☐
c) Prepare several different selling angles ☐
d) See what happens and leave it to chance ☐

6. What should your attitude to jargon be?
a) Use it to disguise what I do ☐
b) Never use it ☐
c) Use a bit ☐
d) Use a lot ☐

7. What's the best way to get business?
a) Tell them you are available ☐
b) Tell them you are all booked up at the moment ☐
c) Be evasive ☐
d) Be unclear and say maybe ☐

8. In a well-supplied market, what's the best thing to do?
a) Offer the same as everyone else ☐
b) Offer anything they want ☐
c) Go with the flow ☐
d) Try selling the opposite of everyone else ☐

9. What's the best way to reassure a customer?
a) It's difficult (but you can fix it) ☐
b) It's difficult (and it will cost more) ☐
c) It's simple (because you are experienced) ☐
d) It's simple (and it will be cheap) ☐

10. What's the best way to secure a deal on the phone?
a) Start discounting immediately ☐
b) State your price clearly and don't deviate ☐
c) Change price during the call, based on what they say ☐
d) Be vague about your prices ☐

FRIDAY

How to conduct yourself

So far we've covered many of the emotional and practical aspects of running your own business. There is, however, another essential element that books cannot really teach you but which requires careful attention nonetheless. It is not tangible. You can't buy it, quantify it or measure it. You may acquire skills that allow you to believe that you have got 'it' about right, although you'll never know for sure. This elusive element is the way you conduct yourself.

When you start your own business, the way you come across to others is paramount. Within seconds, you can convey completely the wrong impression. Your manners, your dress and your attitude therefore all count for a great deal. You can lose the interest or respect of your potential customer in an instant, so you owe it to yourself to consider carefully what sort of image you wish to convey.

Today we are going to look at:

- how to create a 'company culture' when you run your own business
- why you should only do business with people you like
- how to motivate yourself
- what to do and what not to do.

You *are* the company culture

You need to confront the fact that, when you run your own business, you *are* the company culture. There are no hazy mission statements to fall back on, there's no human resources department, and there's no glossy brochure to cover up for shoddy behaviour. You need to behave as you would like others to behave. What does that mean?

Disregarding personal style for a moment, there are some basic principles of good conduct to which you should adhere. Here are some examples.

- Be polite.
- Be realistic.
- Turn up on time.
- Return calls when you say you will.
- Pay your bills immediately.
- Over-deliver if you wish, but never under-deliver.

You can create your own list based on your personal preferences and the nature of your business. Over time, you will undoubtedly receive back as much good behaviour as you dish out. You will gain a reputation for high standards, integrity and honesty. Repeat business will follow.

To put it another way, if you are small-minded, you will lose good customers and attract those who are also small-minded and unreliable. You need to map out at an early stage what you believe to be the important parts of how to conduct your business. Then use that as a blueprint to determine how you should conduct *yourself*, and in turn what you expect and desire of others. This will stand you in good stead when you have to confront a dilemma about whether to decline some business, or if you have to take the harsh decision to inform an existing customer that you will no longer work with them.

Only do business with people you like

This is quite a tricky area but it really is worth spending time on working out how you feel about your business relationships. Naturally, if you work in a service business or run a retail outlet, you can't vet everybody with whom you have a transaction, but you *can* choose the nature of your suppliers and associates. As you develop your own personal style you will become better at working out what other people are like to deal with. Eventually, you should be in a position whereby it is you who chooses to do business with somebody, not the other way round.

This is important because, ultimately, if you don't enjoy the company of the people with whom you have to interact, you will effectively have engineered a state of affairs in which you don't like what you do. This is a disaster for anyone who runs their own business. Indeed, the whole point of starting your own business is to design a set-up that suits your particular style.

Of course, sometimes it takes a while for someone to show their true colours, and there will be times when somebody you really like lets you down. Unfortunately, there is nothing you can do about this, and it is undoubtedly true that any disappointments will be felt harder by you as an individual than by companies in the collective sense. However, in the long run your judgement will improve with experience, and your goal should be only to do business with the people you like.

Don't distinguish between tasks

It's human nature to say, 'I love doing X' and 'I hate doing Y'. Sadly, now that you are your own boss, you need to stop making the distinction between the two. Because it was your decision to go it alone, whatever needs doing now has to be done by you and is ultimately entirely for your personal benefit. Even if the task is working out how much tax to pay, it is worth doing well because, if you don't, you'll be the one to lose out.

It's also often inaccurate to presuppose that something you expect to be unpleasant will actually turn out to be so. In reality, the outcome of a situation that you are anxious about is frequently the opposite of what you expect it to be. This may sound false but it is actually true, as the examples in the box below illustrate.

Unexpected outcomes

Can you imagine how you might have a better meeting firing someone than giving them a pay rise?

The firing

Employer: 'I'm very sorry but after a lot of discussion and anxiety I'm afraid we can't keep you in this job any longer.'

Employee: 'I can't say I'm surprised. I haven't been coping very well and I haven't been happy. I was thinking of going travelling instead.'

The pay rise

Employer: 'I am pleased to tell you that we have agreed a £3,000 pay rise for you.'

Employee: 'I'm really disappointed. I was expecting a minimum of £5,000.'

The supposedly disagreeable cold call looming on your checklist might well be the very thing that makes you most happy this month. Go on. Get to it!

Remember the positive things you've done

It's a knack to be able to stay positive. All people who start their own business suffer from some form of self-doubt from time to time. Since you don't have colleagues congratulating you on a job well done, you need to generate your own humble form of self-congratulation. No one else is going to bother, so find a private way to celebrate your successes and keep your confidence levels up. Consider these ideas for reminding yourself that you are pretty good at what you do and so you deserve a pat on the back:

- Write down your income.
- Write down your profit.
- Say out loud: 'I'm still in business.'
- Choose your favourite recent business transaction.
- Ask a customer if they will write a reference for you.
- Ask your partner or a friend if they think you are any good at what you do.
- Invent an ingenious plan for the near future.
- Calculate whether you can afford a holiday soon.
- Book a holiday.
- If you have rivals, consider whether they are doing as well as you.

Stay positive
Remember this straightforward maxim: **Everything you achieve you've done yourself.**

Principles of good conduct

As well as mapping out some rules for how you will conduct your business, you need to make some rules for how you will conduct *yourself*. Not only will they help you maintain your self-discipline and improve your efficiency but they will also inform your expectations of what standards of conduct you require from others.

Never moan

Moaning is one of the most unattractive features of any personality. Whose company would you prefer? Someone with a positive, optimistic outlook? Or someone who spends the whole time bellyaching about things that aren't going well? Moaning is unacceptable for anyone who runs their own business. This is because it's actually an admission of failure.

This is not an exaggeration. If you run your own business, your fortunes are entirely in your hands. You can invoke as many higher powers as you like, blame macro-economic conditions and invent reams of excuses about precisely why you don't have enough work at the moment. None of this smokescreen will disguise the fact that you haven't had the determination to go and get it. This is not some assertion cooked up by a motivation guru or a sales zealot. It's cold, hard logic.

 TIP **Stick up mantras where you can see them**
For example, type this up and stick it on the wall:
'No moaning'.

Never drink during the day

Keep a clear head at work. Don't drink. The same goes for drugs and anything else that has the capacity to turn you into a blithering idiot during work hours. Save it for the weekend. If you ever receive a call from a customer in the afternoon and you are less than compos mentis, your reputation will be on the slide immediately. 'I wouldn't use him, he's a bit of a drinker' is not how you would wish to be described around town. If you really do have to have a near-compulsory jolly with a customer one day, turn your mobile off and return any calls when you are sober, saying that unfortunately you were in an all-day meeting or out of town. Never get involved in important business when you are in danger of talking rubbish.

Never finish a day before deciding what to do the next morning

This simple little discipline works incredibly well. It's outstandingly easy to do, and is the best ever way of ensuring a good night's sleep. Just write down what you have to do the next day and, if appropriate, allocate the necessary time for it. Now you can relax. There are many subsidiary benefits to this approach. Firstly, it's impossible to forget to do something, because it is written down. Secondly, you come across as totally on the ball because you genuinely *do* know what you are doing the next day. And, thirdly, you don't have to worry about the tasks for the next day, so you can go and have that drink after all.

Never do anything unless you know why you are doing it

This is a good principle for all business people to abide by. Actually, it applies to anything you ever do in your whole life. It stands to reason. Think carefully about what you are doing and why you are doing it. Your time is your potential money. If you are doing something unnecessary, for every minute you do so you are shooting yourself in the foot. Only do the things that matter. Your time is too precious to approach it any other way.

Have reserve plans for every day

When you start your own business, you may well quite naively assume that the shape of tomorrow will be exactly as it is written in your personal organizer. Nothing could be further from the truth! Just when you have put a suit on, on a day when you think you have three meetings, they may all have been cancelled by 9.30 a.m. If that does happen, it is not acceptable to sit around and do nothing on the grounds that everything has changed. In fact, you should assume every day that everything *will* change.

Being incapable of adapting rapidly is a big warning sign for anyone who works on their own. Expressing dismay that everything has changed at short notice conveys the impression that it is easy to catch you on the hop and that you are a bit of a plodder. Life's a mess – roll with it and enjoy the ride.

What you need are Plans B, C and so on that you can engage immediately when all the other activities fall away. The trick to avoid disappointment is to work out that this *will* happen *before* it happens. Then when it does, which it undoubtedly will, instead of being aghast at this extraordinary development and going into a flat spin, you simply reach for your Plan B file.

Remember Plan B

The wonderful thing about Plan B is that Plan B is often more productive than Plan A. Here are some examples of things that anyone can do to generate a Plan B.

1 As a matter of course, read all the trade press related to your business, and that which your potential customers read, plus anything else that stimulates you. Collect ideas and articles, and use them to generate initiatives and give you the basis for a speculative phone call or proposal.

2 If an ex-customer or colleague surfaces somewhere in a new job, call them immediately, keeping an eye out for information on the new market that they have entered. This is how you will extend your customer base beyond its current shape.

3 Have good data sources, become familiar with them, and use them to generate ideas. Remember in particular that trends change all the time, so you cannot claim to be on top of developments if you don't check them regularly.

4 Read more books than your customers. Barely anyone in any industry has ever read what they are supposed to. If you have, you can help by introducing new ideas and by being the authority on a specific subject.

5 When you have achieved something extracurricular, make it part of your CV and sales patter. People are interested, and it adds a human dimension to the person behind the business skills that they are being offered.

6 Constantly rewrite your CV, redefining your skills again and again to reflect what you are best at and what you enjoy doing most. Don't forget that what you are best at and what you enjoy most are often strongly related. This is very much part of the joy of running your own business – you can dictate, within reason, the nature of the work you choose to do and mould it as you develop your understanding of yourself.

7 Regularly examine the shape of your business so that you understand it properly and can explain the facts to your clients. For example:
  - How many clients did you have in year/month 1/2/3?
  - How many jobs did you do in year/month 1/2/3?
  - How much repeat business did you have in year 2?
  - Look at the bottom of your contact list and call everyone below the pester line.

If after all these suggestions you are still able to claim that you have no idea what to do with your time, you should probably not be running your own business. Once you get the hang of it, you will have created your own company culture, and your potential customers will be left in no doubt about what you stand for. It's then up to them to decide whether your style suits them and, if you have conducted yourself well, it is very likely that it will.

'Solitude is the school of genius.'
Edward Gibbon

Summary

Today we've looked at why it pays to remember that you *are* the company culture. How you conduct yourself will ultimately determine how your company is regarded.

If possible, only do business with people you like. This is hard for mass-volume businesses, but do it if you can – you will have a much nicer time. At the same time, don't distinguish between nice and less nice things to do – they all need doing, so just get on with it.

To increase your confidence, remind yourself of all the positive things you've done rather than moaning. Never drink during the day or you are likely to ruin your reputation. Never finish a day before deciding what to do the next morning, and don't do anything unless you know why you are doing it – you'd be amazed how many people do.

Because nothing ever happens as you expect, have reserve plans for every day. Get used to things changing and do something else, safe in the knowledge that Plan B is often more productive than Plan A. And, of course, don't forget Plans C, D, E and beyond.

SUNDAY

MONDAY

TUESDAY

WEDNESDAY

THURSDAY

FRIDAY

SATURDAY

Fact check [answers at the back]

1. What's your attitude to the culture of your new company?
   a) I'm not too fussed – it doesn't matter ❑
   b) I *am* the company culture ❑
   c) It's conveyed by my marketing materials ❑
   d) It's what my customers make it ❑

2. What's the best approach to customers?
   a) Do business with everyone ❑
   b) Do business with anyone ❑
   c) Do business with people even if you don't like them, and vice versa ❑
   d) Only do business with people you like ❑

3. When faced with a list of things to do, what should you do?
   a) Distinguish between pleasant and unpleasant things to do ❑
   b) Not distinguish between pleasant and unpleasant things to do ❑
   c) Fixate on all the pleasant things and do them first ❑
   d) Fixate on the unpleasant things and put them off ❑

4. When faced with a confidence crisis, what should you do?
   a) Remind yourself of all the positive things you've done ❑
   b) Remind yourself of all the negative things you've done ❑
   c) Decide to give up on the basis that you are no good ❑
   d) Pour your heart out to anyone who will listen ❑

5. When things go wrong, what's the worst thing you can do?
   a) Say it's just business ❑
   b) Laugh it off ❑
   c) Moan about it ❑
   d) Try to fix it ❑

6. The pubs are open during working hours, so when do you go for a drink?
   a) 11 a.m. ❑
   b) 1 p.m. ❑
   c) 5.30 p.m. ❑
   d) Never ❑

7. When it's time to leave work, what should you do?
   a) Drop everything and head out of the door ❑
   b) Hang around for a bit, then go ❑
   c) Decide what to do the next morning before leaving ❑
   d) Stay for another two hours worrying about tomorrow ❑

8. What's the best approach to deciding whether to do something?
   a) Just do it ❑
   b) Ignore it ❑
   c) Think about it and then ignore it ❑
   d) Only do it once you know why you are doing it ❑

9. What's your attitude to having reserve plans for every day?
a) It's a poor idea – I haven't got time ❑
b) It's a bad idea – I never need them ❑
c) It's a great idea in case things change ❑
d) It's a good idea but I won't get round to it ❑

10. Do you agree that Plan B is often more productive than Plan A?
a) Yes ❑
b) No ❑
c) Sometimes ❑
d) I don't have a Plan B ❑

SUNDAY

MONDAY

TUESDAY

WEDNESDAY

THURSDAY

FRIDAY

SATURDAY

Setting up reminders and tripwires

If you know you're not very good at something, anticipating that difficulty by putting reminders and 'tripwires' in place will help you do it more effectively. Not only will reminders help you get things done but they will allow you to engineer the time and space to generate great ideas and improve all aspects of your business.

It's easy to panic and waste time if you don't have a backup, and tripwires will allow you to line this up. Instead of trying to do everything at once, doing things in sequence – tackling the simple jobs first and fast – will liberate time for more complex tasks. Think carefully before you rush into something. What effect will your action have? Is that what you want? Is it worth doing? It takes only seconds to work these things out.

Today we are going to look at:

- how to trip yourself up on purpose
- why writing it down gets it done
- setting up business planning tripwires
- ways to save time
- multitasking versus rapid sequential tasking
- putting the effort in only where it gets you somewhere.

Trip yourself up on purpose

'If you're going to do something, go start.
Life's simpler than we sometimes can admit.'

Robert De Niro

If you know you are not very good at something, do something now to anticipate that difficulty and increase your effectiveness when the time comes. By now you have done a lot of thinking, so decide how precisely you are going to implement the great ideas you've generated. We don't want them languishing on a piece of paper in a drawer somewhere and never seeing the light of day. Getting them done will require a mixture of business effort and personal effort. It is all about setting up 'tripwires' so that you cannot fail to action something.

Many of us know that, if we don't write something down, we will most likely forget it. That could be a sticky note on the back of the door saying 'don't forget keys', a shopping list or a note on the steering wheel saying 'oil' or 'petrol'. This is the principle behind tripwires. We work out what will go wrong *before* it does, and put the measures in place to prevent that from happening. To make this really effective, you need to find out how everything works, and work out where it's most likely to fall down. Predict that, and you will ensure that the important things get done.

Discussing broad concepts in their embryonic phase can be fun, particularly for those who don't have to get the thing in question done. But nothing irritates a decent businessperson more than a good idea that hasn't quite seen the light of day. No one cares why; the point is, it's still on the drawing board and the fruits of it have not been realized.

Often this is because there is confusion about whose responsibility it actually is. At other times it's because the idea is allowed to drift and no one pushes for any particular deadline to be met. The trick is to write it down. If you intend to start, then start. It's that simple.

Business planning tripwires

Broad questions to ask yourself when designing business planning tripwires include the following:

1 What, ultimately, do I want for my business?
2 By when do I want it?
3 How exactly am I going to get there?
4 Do I need help and, if so, from whom?
5 Have I started yet?

The precise list of what needs to be done will depend on what ideas you come up with and what matters most to your business, but these are the underlying questions to ask when planning tripwires.

Use the answers to these questions when setting up specific tripwires. Here are some examples of questions to ask yourself next. You can customize them to reflect your own circumstances.

● What will make me get this done?
● Is that bulletproof or too flimsy?

- Does that allow me to wriggle out of it later?
- If so, what sanction will force me to do it?
- Have I actually put that in place right now?

There is no room for excuses because it is entirely in your interests to get this done, even if it does lie in the future.

This technique works for specific items, but it also works for the overall shape of your business (and for your personal life too). If that is an exercise that you would find useful, then you might want to write down your one-year, three-year, five-year and ten-year aims. The timespans don't matter but the principle does. Choose frequencies appropriate to your business, and write down the answers to the questions.

The world is full of people who claim to have plenty of ideas but, strangely, haven't quite started to realize them. Don't allow yourself to be one of these people. Get started immediately, and learn as you go. If one tripwire doesn't work for you, you can always change it along the way, but don't fall into the trap of standing around pontificating when you could be using the time to get the thing done.

Dropping grenades in fishponds

Explosive ideas don't occur by themselves. You need to create time and space to invent clever interventions that will make your business a success. Some people need a severe shock to force them to do something, so here is a form of disaster planning – we will call them grenades – that may help catapult you into action. 'Dropping grenades in fishponds' involves deliberately imagining extreme scenarios in order to jolt yourself into doing the necessary thing.

The purpose of these questions is not to scare you senseless and prevent you from sleeping well. It is to highlight the important issues that may well occur at some point in the future.

Idea grenades include:

- What if this were the only idea available?
- What if it never happened?
- What if there were 20 more like this?

You can see how this extreme line of questioning pushes everything that bit further. Go a bit over the top to test your mettle. If this were the only idea you had, would you still do it? There's no point in wasting time on tripwires and implementation if you aren't convinced, and, if you aren't, then why should your colleagues or customers be?

Personal grenades include:

- What if I could never work again?
- What if I took a year off?
- What if I quit this and did something totally different?

These are pretty poignant too, and the intention is to make you stop and think so that you can work out the severity of an item and how badly you want to do it. Then, if you conclude that it definitely does matter, you can engineer the necessary tripwires.

Business grenades include:

- What if the business folded tomorrow?
- What if all the staff walked out?
- What if all our customers suddenly disappeared?

Scorched-earth scenarios like this are very polarizing and are good for helping you clarify your thoughts so that you really know what you are trying to achieve. Use this approach to determine how badly something matters, and how you are going to guarantee that it gets done.

Line up your backup

Whether it's suppliers or human resource, you always need a backup, so line this up before there is a short-term panic. The principle here is that small actions and reminders yield big results. It just depends how severe a memory jog you require, and only you can be the judge of that. If you are quite efficient, then you may not need any of these measures at all. If you have trouble with motivation, or you are a bit disorganized, then you may well do. Put the appropriate number of tripwires in place, but don't overdo it to the point that they are constantly preventing you from doing the task in hand. They are there to make you do things, not to stop you from doing them. If you put too many in place, you will be damming up the river to see how it flows – pointless.

Don't replace the original, replace the spare

You can apply simple principles that save time in your working day, week or year. One of these is: don't replace the original, replace the spare. This is an extension of the 'successful people buy in bulk' idea. Every good chef knows that you need a spare of everything, so that when you run out of the original, you simply reach for it and the meal still happens. Many people in life never have a spare, so whenever they run out of something there is a panic. They then either rush about in a mad flap to buy another item, thus increasing their stress, or the meal doesn't happen. The analogy applies equally to those in business. Whether it is supplies or human resource, you always need a spare. When the spare is used up, buy another spare. Don't replace the original, replace the spare.

Multitasking versus rapid sequential tasking

Getting a lot done is often associated with multitasking, and there has been a lot of discussion recently about whether everyone is able to do it. The evidence suggests that women are better at multitasking than men, so if you are male and therefore no good at multitasking, try doing 'rapid sequential tasking' instead. This is when, if you can't cope with doing everything at once, you do things one at a time, in a sequence. Do simple tasks first and fast, and then liberate time for more complex tasks. This is often a good idea even if you are good at multitasking.

Everyone has checklists, and they usually contain a curious mixture of important and trivial things to do. Strip out the easy trivia from the important stuff, and rattle through them sequentially and quickly. Don't have several things on the go at once. Only start the next thing when you have finished the previous one. Just because guys apparently can't 'do' multitasking doesn't mean they can't do rapid sequential tasking.

 Do tasks in your own way
Part of the knack of making sure things get done is realizing what you are actually capable of doing. If you can only do one thing at a time, do it fast and move on to the next thing.

Decide when to put the effort in

Think carefully before you rush into something. What effect will your action have? Is that what you want? Is it worth doing? It takes only a few seconds to work out whether your efforts will get you anywhere. Your ability to get things done is one thing but whether you are doing the *right* things in the first place is a completely different matter. Any good businessperson will tell you that you need to develop the knack of working out whether you are pursuing the right opportunities, and deciding how much time and effort to spend on them.

One of the hardest decisions to make is to pull out of something when you have invested a lot of physical and emotional energy into it. But pull out is precisely what you must do if the thing in question is going nowhere. Try again by all means, but don't keep repeating the same mistakes or misjudgements. Alternatively, you might conclude that you can't do something but that someone else can.

Summary

Today we've looked at ways to trip yourself up on purpose so that, if you know you are not good at something, you can anticipate the difficulty and increase your effectiveness when the time comes. Design your tripwires now to enhance your ability to get things done.

Ask yourself the right questions to jolt you into doing what's necessary. Write down what you need to do and it's more likely that you'll do it. Generate reminders to make time and space to create clever interventions that will ignite your business. Try rapid sequential tasking instead of trying to do everything at once: doing simple jobs first and fast will free up time for more complex tasks.

With suppliers and human resource, you'll always need backup, so line this up before there is a panic. Before you rush into something, think carefully about the consequences and put the effort in only where it gets you somewhere.

Implementing these ideas will help you save time and make you more efficient, creative and productive in all aspects of your business.

Fact-check [answers at the back]

1. If you persistently fail to do things, what's the best thing to do?
   a) Live with it – some things never change ☐
   b) Ignore it – it doesn't matter ☐
   c) Arrange to trip yourself up on purpose ☐
   d) Make a New Year's resolution ☐

2. If a tripwire doesn't work after a week, what should you do?
   a) Change it for another one ☐
   b) Admit you're no good at this stuff ☐
   c) Abandon it – it's clearly not working ☐
   d) Persuade someone else to help ☐

3. Something needs doing within a fortnight, but not straight away. What do you do?
   a) Leave it till the time comes ☐
   b) Assume you'll remember ☐
   c) Ignore it – there are more urgent things to do ☐
   d) Put it in your personal organizer so you can't forget ☐

4. What should you do if 20 things to do come in on the same day?
   a) Write some down and then give up with the rest ☐
   b) Write each one down as they come in ☐
   c) Assume you'll remember the first few and then get swamped ☐
   d) Give up immediately and panic ☐

5. You lapse into bad, disorganized ways. What should you do?
   a) Accept it – stuff happens ☐
   b) Impose sanctions on yourself and stick to them ☐
   c) Pretend it never happened ☐
   d) Say you'll try harder next time ☐

6. The business is going well but your personal life is suffering. What should you do?
   a) Try applying some of the same discipline to improve it ☐
   b) Ignore it – it will have to wait ☐
   c) Work even harder ☐
   d) Call a mate and go for a drink ☐

7. Your business is lacking in ideas. What do you do?
   a) Press on anyway ☐
   b) Ask a mate what to do ☐
   c) Detonate some idea 'grenades' and shake things up ☐
   d) Do what you did last year ☐

8. When you run out of printer cartridges, what's the best thing to do?
   a) Curse the fact that you've run out ☐
   b) Send someone rushing to the shop ☐
   c) Blame someone for letting you run out in the first place ☐
   d) Reach calmly for the spare you already have, and then make a note to replace the spare ☐

9. You have 20 things to do today. What should you do?
a) Start five of them at the same time ❏
b) Do whatever one you want and then get distracted ❏
c) Start one, finish it, and then move on to another ❏
d) Panic and put the kettle on ❏

10. When something isn't working, what's the right approach?
a) Try again – it might work this time ❏
b) Get someone else to have a go ❏
c) Forget it and do something else ❏
d) Change your approach ❏

7 × 7

1 Seven important thoughts

- **Thinking is free, so do it more often.** 'I haven't had time to think.' How many times have we heard that said? It is your job to create the appropriate time to think.
- **The next big thing might be small.** When you run a business, there is great mileage to be had from lots of little ideas. Little ideas are great. They are less hard to come up with than big ideas, they are usually cheaper and easier to implement, and they can be done more quickly.
- **Nip into the gap.** You need to be dexterous enough to nip into the gaps that other businesses might have missed by being too cautious. Be flexible and keep coming up with new ideas. Don't be scared to change if you spot a new opportunity.
- **Make over-delivery an exception.** Many owner-managers are so desperate to please that they over-deliver hugely on every job. However, in truth, over-delivery equates to underpayment.
- **Vary your working day.** As Benjamin Franklin said, 'The definition of insanity is doing the same thing over and over again and expecting different results'. Eventually, we all get bored if we have to do the same thing for long periods. To remain positive, move on to new things whenever possible.
- **Don't 'do gloomy'.** No one wants to listen to someone moaning. The circumstances might be difficult but you don't have to be miserable. Adopt a positive attitude and concentrate on what can be done, rather than what the obstacles are.
- **You only need one girlfriend.** Complaining that there is no work is like a man saying there are no women in his town. You only need one girlfriend or piece of work, so go and find it.

2 Seven lucky money questions

- Could you do without offices by working from home?
- If you cannot work from home, is there an elegant alternative?
- Could you operate without a formal business partner?
- Could you have less prescribed arrangements where you can bring help in as and when work dictates?
- Could you survive without delegating anything?
- With a little ingenuity and re-engineering, could you do everything you need yourself?
- Could you pay yourself less for a while?

If the answer is yes to any or all of these, you can have a near-infinite margin.

3 Seven stars

- **James Dyson** – In the late 1970s Dyson had the idea of using cyclonic separation to create a vacuum cleaner that would not lose suction as it picked up dirt. After five years and many prototypes, Dyson developed the G-Force cleaner, but no one would launch his product in the UK as it would disturb the valuable cleaner-bag market, so in June 1993 he set up his own manufacturing company and research centre. His product now outsells those of some of the companies that rejected his idea. Dyson's story is a classic: a bright idea followed by years of dedication in the face of rejection from the powers that be. His fortune is now estimated at £1.1 billion.

- **Tom Peters** – Tom is the doyen of business gurus, having written the classic *In Search Of Excellence* (1982) with his partner Robert Waterman. He identified the basic principles of how to run a successful business and stay ahead of the competition. These included a bias for action (get out there and try something), stay close to the customer (don't be distracted by the internal stuff) and be hands-on and value-driven (top companies make meaning, not just money) – all of which is food for thought when starting a business.

- **Michael Dell** – While a student at the University of Texas, Dell started an informal business upgrading computers at home. Not having the overhead of a computer store, he applied for and won a vendor licence to bid for contracts for the State of Texas. In January 1984 he registered his company as 'PCs Limited'. Operating out of a condominium, the business initially sold around $80,000 in upgraded PCs, kits and add-on components. After relocating to a business centre, he employed some order takers, a few more people to fulfil them, and a manufacturing staff (in his own words) 'consisting of three guys with screwdrivers sitting at six-foot tables'. The venture's capitalization cost was just $1,000.

  In 1992 at the age of 27, Dell became the youngest CEO to have his company ranked in *Fortune* magazine's list of the top 500 corporations. Dell bucked pretty much every system previously set up in the computer industry while setting up a new one of his own: stripping out all the overhead and dealing direct with customers to provide them with customized products.

- **Ingvar Kamprad** – As a young boy, Kamprad developed a business selling matches to neighbours from his bicycle. He found that he could buy them in bulk very cheaply, sell them individually at a low price and still make a good profit. From this modest base he expanded into selling fish, Christmas tree decorations, seeds and ballpoint pens. When he was 17, his father gave him a cash reward for succeeding in his studies, and he used the money to establish what has grown into IKEA. According to one Swedish business magazine he is the wealthiest person in the world, although this is based on the assumption that he owns the entire company, a fact that both he and IKEA dispute.

- **Ricardo Semler** – Semler is internationally famous for creating the world's most unusual workplace. His management philosophy of empowering employees and looking at corporate structures in new ways is a constant challenge to the ingrained models of the corporate pyramid. At his company Semco, workers choose their own bosses. Financial information is shared with everyone. A high percentage of the employees determine their own salaries and self-managed teams replace hierarchy and procedure. Two spare seats are always kept free at every board meeting for any member of staff to attend. When there is an issue, one of his favourite approaches is to do nothing on the grounds that common sense will eventually prevail. He has appeared on television all over the world and has lectured to over 500 audiences. He has been chosen as a global leader by the World Economic Forum, *Fortune* magazine and Dow Jones.

- **Lakshmi Mittal** – The chairman and Chief Executive of ArcelorMittal, the world's largest steelmaking company, Mittal started his career working in the family's steelmaking business in India. In 1976 he set out to establish its international division, beginning with the buying of a run-down plant in Indonesia. He pioneered the development of integrated mini-mills and the use of direct reduced iron as a scrap substitute for steelmaking, and led the consolidation of the steel industry. Mittal Steel now has shipments of 42.1 million tons of steel and profits in the billions. This success did not happen overnight. Four decades of growth are testament to the durability of his vision. Depending on which survey you read, Mittal is the richest man in Europe and the fifth richest in the world, with a personal wealth of £19 billion. The *Financial Times* named him Person of the Year in 2006, and in 2007 he was named one of the 100 Most Influential People by *Time* magazine.

- **Richard Branson** – In 1966 Branson launched his first successful business – a magazine called *Student*. By 1970 he had started selling records by mail order and he opened his first record shop on London's Oxford Street in 1971. The Virgin Records label was launched two years later and subsequent decades saw the company grow into what is now one of the most successful businesses in the world.

  Throughout, Branson has demonstrated a knack for applying his personal style to a bewildering array of business sectors. The group's company statement explains: 'Contrary to what some people may think, our constantly expanding and eclectic empire is neither random nor reckless. Each successive venture demonstrates our devotion to picking the right market and the right opportunity. When we start a new venture, we base it on hard research and analysis. We ask fundamental questions: is this an opportunity for restructuring a market and creating competitive advantage? Is the customer confused or badly served? Is this an opportunity for building the Virgin Brand? Can we add value?' Branson believes that if you have faith in yourself anything can be done. He recommends that you live life to the full and never give up – wise words indeed for those starting businesses.

4 Seven great quotes

- 'The beginning is half of every action.' *Greek proverb*
- 'The first step to getting the things you want out of life is this: decide what you want.' *Ben Stein*
- 'We have no money so we will have to think.' *Lord Rutherford*
- 'Never be afraid to tell the world who you are.' *Anon.*
- 'Sell the crunch not the apple.' *Anon.*
- 'Solitude is the school of genius.' *Edward Gibbon*
- 'If you're going to do something, go start. Life's simpler than we sometimes can admit.' *Robert De Niro*

5 Seven things to do today

- Get started.
- Line up the right tools for the job.
- Have a clear view on the money.
- Publicize what you are doing.
- Make some calls.
- Draw up your own code of conduct.
- Set up reminders and tripwires.

6 Seven deadly sins

- Overcomplicating things
- Putting things off
- Poor communication, or none at all
- Fudging money issues
- Ignoring or putting off tough decisions
- Unreliable people
- Moaning

7 Seven of the best resources

- **The Prince's Trust** provides advice on grants and starting up. www.princestrust.org.uk
- **Fresh Business Thinking** is an online resource for entrepreneurial small businesses, with lots of start-up advice. www.freshbusinessthinking.com
- **The National Federation of Enterprise Agencies** (the Small Business Administration in the US) explains how businesses can get started and provides independent and impartial advice, training and mentoring to new and emerging businesses. www.nfea.com; www.sba.gov
- **The UK Intellectual Property Office** (the Patent and Trademark Office in the US) gives advice on how to define and protect your idea if it is unique, and can help you get the right type of protection for your creation or invention. www.ipo.gov.uk; www.uspto.gov
- **Small Business** offers advice for start-up companies, guides and tips on starting a business, raising finance, business grants and loans, and managing staff. www.smallbusiness.co.uk
- **Business Balls** offers advice on how to write a business plan and free templates that you can download and fill in. www.businessballs.com
- **The Health and Safety Executive** in the UK (the Occupational Safety and Health Administration in the US) explains health and safety legislation and tells you what you need to consider as an employer. www.hse.gov.uk/legislation; www.osha.gov

Answers

Sunday: 1a; 2c; 3c; 4d; 5c; 6a; 7c; 8b; 9a; 10d.

Monday: 1c; 2a; 3a; 4d; 5c; 6d; 7b; 8a; 9c; 10b.

Tuesday: 1d; 2a; 3b; 4d; 5a; 6b; 7c; 8c; 9d; 10a.

Wednesday: 1a; 2d; 3b; 4c; 5a; 6b; 7d; 8a; 9b; 10b.

Thursday: 1d; 2a; 3b; 4b; 5c; 6b; 7a; 8d; 9c; 10b.

Friday: 1b; 2d; 3b; 4a; 5c; 6d; 7c; 8d; 9c; 10a.

Saturday: 1c; 2a; 3d; 4b; 5b; 6a; 7c; 8d; 9c; 10d.

ALSO AVAILABLE IN THE 'IN A WEEK' SERIES

APPRAISALS • BRAND MANAGEMENT • BUSINESS PLANS • CONTENT MARKETING • COVER LETTERS • DIGITAL MARKETING • DIRECT MARKETING • EMOTIONAL INTELLIGENCE • FINDING & HIRING TALENT • JOB HUNTING • LEADING TEAMS • MARKET RESEARCH • MARKETING • MBA • MOBILE MARKETING • NETWORKING • OUTSTANDING CONFIDENCE • PEOPLE MANAGEMENT • PLANNING YOUR CAREER • PROJECT MANAGEMENT • SMALL BUSINESS MARKETING • STARTING A NEW JOB • TACKLING TOUGH INTERVIEW QUESTIONS • TIME MANAGEMENT

For information about other titles in the 'In A Week' series, please visit www.teachyourself.co.uk

MORE TITLES AVAILABLE IN THE 'IN A WEEK' SERIES

ADVANCED NEGOTIATION SKILLS • ASSERTIVENESS • BUSINESS ECONOMICS • COACHING • COPYWRITING • DECISION MAKING • DIFFICULT CONVERSATIONS • ECOMMERCE • FINANCE FOR NON-FINANCIAL MANAGERS • JOB INTERVIEWS • MANAGING STRESS AT WORK • MANAGING YOUR BOSS • MANAGING YOURSELF • MINDFULNESS AT WORK • NEGOTIATION SKILLS • NLP • PEOPLE SKILLS • PSYCHOMETRIC TESTING • SEO AND SEARCH MARKETING • SOCIAL MEDIA MARKETING • START YOUR OWN BUSINESS • STRATEGY • SUCCESSFUL SELLING • UNDERSTANDING AND INTERPRETING ACCOUNTS

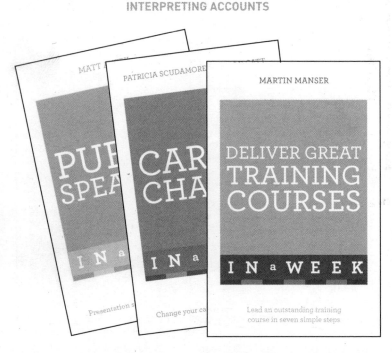

For information about other titles in the 'In A Week' series, please visit www.teachyourself.co.uk

twenty-five years, who inspires me still. As my research for this book consisted mostly of conversation and observation, I thank my parents, Judy and Phil; my brothers, Todd and Curt; Kelley (my sister-friend); and Sherry and Joyce, my two oldest and dearest friends. Thanks as well to my husband's family, and to the many friends, not all of them wives, or even women, with whom I've shared confidence over the years, and who contributed to the story of *The Wife's Tale* in ways they couldn't know.

Once again, I owe a debt to southwestern Ontario, in whose memory I find Baldoon County. Finally, I wish to thank my tribe in southern California, the group of mothers from a Topanga school who welcomed this transplanted Canadian into their fold as I wrote the story of an outsider searching for her place.

www.virago.co.uk

virago

To find out more about Lori Lansens and
other Virago authors, visit:
www.virago.co.uk

Visit the Virago website for:

- Exclusive features and interviews with authors,
  including Margaret Atwood, Maya Angelou,
  Sarah Waters and Nina Bawden

- News of author events and forthcoming titles

- Competitions

- Exclusive signed copies

- Discounts on new publications

- Book-group guides

- Free extracts from a wide range of titles

PLUS: subscribe to our free monthly newsletter

RUSH HOME ROAD
Lori Lansens

'Sharla didn't know how long she'd been sitting there when
the door screeched open behind her. She held her breath
knowing this was the beginning and the end of her life.'

Sharla Cody is only five but has already had a troubled
life – only to find herself dumped with Addy, an elderly
neighbour, when her mother takes off for the summer. Two
very unlikely people are about to transform each other's
lives forever.

'*Rush Home Road*, the story of a seventy-year-old woman's
journey through the nearly unbearable sorrows of her past,
in order to save an abandoned little girl, is a first novel of
exquisite power, honesty and conviction. Its portrait of how
much has changed, and how little, over nearly a century, in
the realms of race, love, hate and loss, is quite nearly
without flaws' Jacquelyn Mitchard, author of *The Deep
End of the Ocean*

THE GIRLS
Lori Lansens

'I promise: you will never forget this extraordinary story'
Isabel Allende

In twenty-nine years, Rose Darlen has never spent a
moment apart from her twin sister, Ruby. She has never
gone for a solitary walk or had a private conversation. Yet,
in all that time, she has never once looked into Ruby's eyes.
Joined at the head, 'The Girls' (as they are known in their
small town) attempt to lead a normal life, but can't help
being extraordinary. Now almost thirty, Rose and Ruby are
on the verge of becoming the oldest living craniopagus
twins in history, but they are remarkable for a lot more
than their unusual sisterly bond.

You can order other Virago titles through our website: *www.virago.co.uk*
or by using the order form below

☐ Rush Home Road   Lori Lansens   £7.99

☐ The Girls   Lori Lansens   £7.99

The prices shown above are correct at time of going to press. However, the publishers
reserve the right to increase prices on covers from those previously advertised, without
further notice.

_____   🍎   _____

Please allow for postage and packing: **Free UK delivery.**
Europe: add 25% of retail price; Rest of World: 45% of retail price.

To order any of the above or any other Virago titles, please call our credit
card orderline or fill in this coupon and send/fax it to:

Virago, PO Box 121, Kettering, Northants NN14 4ZQ
Fax: 01832 733076   Tel: 01832 737526
Email: aspenhouse@FSBDial.co.uk

☐ I enclose a UK bank cheque made payable to Virago for £ . . . .
☐ Please charge £ . . . . . . to my Visa/Delta/Maestro

Expiry Date | | | | | Maestro Issue No. | | |

NAME (BLOCK LETTERS please) . . . .

ADDRESS . . . .

. . . .

. . . .

Postcode . . . . Telephone . . . .

Signature . . . .

Please allow 28 days for delivery within the UK. Offer subject to price and availability.